Well Done! A fascinating story of achi

Former Executive Director of the Ontario Arts Council and Author

W. Ian Walker's passion for the arts speaks forcefully in this journal of personal courage and discovery.

—Robert Cooper, C.M.,
Toronto Conductor and Choral Educator

A truly courageous journey of many challenges and impressive achievements, proving it can be done!

—Mary Morrison, O.C.,
Canadian Legendary Vocal Performer and Educator

An inspiring story in which vocal music plays a key role! I am very proud of Ian for all his accomplishments and continued dedication to the arts in Canada.

—Adrianne Pieczonka, O.C.,
Canadian and International Soprano

Bravo, Ian! As well as presenting a strong argument for arts education in schools, your story of dedication and determination is a testament to the power of faith, friendship, and music.

—John Fanning, C.M.,
Canadian and International Baritone

This book is the story of overcoming challenges and developing talent into a very fruitful life through the wonderful grace of a personal connection with Jesus Christ.

—Nancy Honeytree-Miller,
First Lady of Jesus Movement Music

W. Ian Walker has written an honest and stirring account of triumph over adversity. Ian's dedication to the arts and to his faith shine through this inspirational autobiography. Highly recommended!

—Dr. Kathleen Garay,
(Retired) McMaster University

Gratitude and perseverance describe Ian's journey from a childhood of 'being different' to the adult discovery of a learning disability that impacted relationships and career opportunities. The diagnosis of ADHD and encounters with the Holy Spirit provided a new lens through which to view past hurts and to anticipate the future with hope and a song in his heart.

—Dr. Carol A. Wood,
(Retired) Ecumenical Chaplain, McMaster University

This is a book that balances a breezy, conversational style and tone with subject matter that is deeply important. W. Ian Walker's engaging narrative carries us through the highs and lows of what is an extraordinary personal journey to triumph over personal adversity with ADHD. One would expect the extremely challenging setbacks and years of hardship that Ian recounts would have turned him bitter. Remarkably, they did not. Fortified by faith, Ian's voice is buoyant, cheerful, and encouraging.

—Richard M. Landau, M.A.,
Media Communications Executive

It is an honour to write this endorsement for a story that will stir the hearts of even the most discouraged. With God, there is always a way to victory. In the midst of constant ups and downs in Ian's life, he has learned a deep secret—sing your way into joyful purpose! Though Ian struggles with short-term memory due to ADHD, a failed marriage, financial pressures, and more, God has stirred his soul. Ian is captured by the One who will not let him go. There is a prophetic flow throughout the pages of this book, and I trust you will feel that flow and respond to that same call to live.

—Jeremy Sinnott,
Worship Leader & Pastor, Catch the Fire Ministries

I've known W. Ian for almost twenty years. Ian was created by God to express joy. As with all who have special assignments in life, the journey in getting there is not always easy. Ian has persevered and continues to be a man who sees the best in life. I believe you will receive hope for your journey by reading Ian's story.

—Steve Long, Senior Leader,
Catch the Fire Toronto

Dear Maria,

So glad that you could be a part of this wonderful day!
for I learn many new things about me's my ADHD! What
is so important to me is my forever friendship with Louise.
We are pals for life!

10/11/18

Many blessings & good health
Ian.

STIRRING
MY
SOUL
TO
Sing

STIRRING
MY
SOUL
TO
Sing

OVERCOMING ADHD THROUGH SONG

W. IAN WALKER

FOREWORD BY NANCY HONEYTREE-MILLER,
FIRST LADY OF JESUS MOVEMENT MUSIC

DEDICATION

To Elaine: Without your love and support, this book would not have been written. Thank you for giving me the time to write combined with your many prayers. I love you very much!

To Bill and Doreen Walker: Thank you for never giving up on your creative son! You always encouraged me to explore my artistic dreams and aspirations from a young child. Mom and Dad, we miss and love you and know that Heaven awaits all who are believers in Christ. Thank you to all Walker and Kawai family members for your constant love, prayers, and additional support.

CONTENTS

ACKNOWLEDGEMENTS

To Jesus Christ, my Lord and Saviour: Thank you for giving me the strength to endure these many years of ADHD. Without this learning disorder, I would not know how to hear your voice or represent your heart. I pray that you will intensify this "life's journey" through this book. You are providing opportunities for Elaine and me to share our life stories as two disabled people being made "one and complete in you."

To the late Catherine Visseau and the late Craig Sproats, the late Judy and Hy Sarick, Ruth and the late Allan Perks, and the late Walter and Ida Pitman, Darrell and Susan Bevan, Carrie Drake, Virginia Henderson Caldwell, Gary and Jill Jones, Marie Patenaude, Michael Rutledge, Cheryl and Leon Sebrins, Joanne Wallgren, Robert and Megan Cooper, Gordon and Shirley MacDonald, Louise Von Massow, Nancy Honeytree-Miller, John and Carol Arnott, Mary-Audrey Raycroft, Steve and Sandra Long, Mel and Susan Natagoc, Jeremy and Connie Sinnott, Dennis and Katie Weidrick, Lisa and Robert Cowling, plus all of our Hamilton Christian

Fellowship Church family, Catch The Fire, and Partners in Harvest Church Network and the Board of Directors for the Youth Choir for the Nations: Thank you all for your ongoing support!

To the late Debbie Reynolds: Growing up I always enjoyed the movie-musical, *The Unsinkable Molly Brown*. Debbie Reynolds was truly "unsinkable" and a true survivor herself, personally and professionally, and was someone I greatly admired. For over fifty years, Debbie dealt with many ups and downs in her personal and professional life. She had family members who dealt with mental issues, and she was actively involved in raising awareness and financial support for this needed community.

To Sandi Patty Peslis: Thank you, Sandi, for being a good friend, mentor, and professor to me. I greatly admire and appreciate all your vocal abilities and talents, your outgoing personality, and your willingness to be involved with the next generation of worship leaders. You have been a vocal mentor to me for so many years! I can't believe that it has now been thirty plus years that you have been involved with CCM industry and with worship music. I have observed first-hand as you have shared in our communications these scriptural principles of "love, compassion, forgiveness, and acceptance." Sandi, when you shared the following statement with me, it rocked my world and truly set me free. You said, "God is still the God of second chances and of new beginnings, and He is still in the business of setting people free." Amen, Sister! I can't wait to see where God is going to "re-fire" you in this next, new season of your life.

Special thanks to Daina Doucet, Byron Humphrey, Richard Landau and Joanne Wallgren, my editors. Many thanks to Richard Landau, who gave me some valuable feedback looking at my situations in this book from an ADHD perspective and truthfully commenting on them. Thank you to Tia Scarborough and all the team at World Alive Press for their ongoing prayer support and professional guidance in the publishing of this book.

FOREWORD

I t is a joy to recommend to you this delightful and wonderfully detailed book by W. Ian Walker called *Stirring My Soul to Sing: Overcoming ADHD through Song.*

Ian and his wife, Elaine, have become my friends since we worked together on the Praising Him in Many Languages Concert, Christmas, 2006. What a joy it was to meet Ian and Elaine and work with his awesome Youth Choir for the Nations Canada, which is comprised mostly of South East Asian children and young adults. We performed my song, "Call of the Harvest," in English and Urdu, not only in the praise concert, but on national Canadian television—*100 Huntley Street.* Wow! What a privilege!

I was very excited when Ian phoned me in early 2006 to ask me to come to Canada to sing in Urdu, the official language of Pakistan. Singing in Urdu had been my passion ever since I had travelled to Pakistan in 2002, learned to sing one of my songs in Urdu, and then made up my mind to make a whole CD for the wonderfully responsive Pakistani

Christians. Thus, when Ian phoned, I was delighted and felt he was an answer to prayer.

Now, once again, it is a surprise and joy to read Ian's book. In many ways we have common experiences—growing up with musical talent but troubled by a lack of fitting in with the popular, social kids. Ian also had the challenge of a learning disability, which was later diagnosed as ADHD. This book is the story of overcoming challenges and developing talent into a very fruitful life through the wonderful grace of a personal connection with Jesus Christ.

Despite the daily harassment Ian endured in both public school and high school, he plunged himself into a rich world of musical talent and training, studying voice, accordion, piano, flute, music theory, choral singing, and drama. He enjoyed a solid Baptist upbringing with a real born again Christian family. His special relationship with his precious grandmother encouraged him to overcome the name calling he received from schoolmates and to keep believing in his musical dreams. As it says in Proverbs 18:16, "*A man's gift ... makes room for him and brings him before great men.*" This book also tells the story of how surviving a car accident helped open the door to a more flowing relationship in Ian's life with the healing power of the Holy Spirit.

Ian is now passing on his wealth of talent and training, along with his living relationship with Jesus, to a terrific group of young people and adults in the Greater Toronto Area. I know that Ian's vision is to welcome other cultures represented in his Youth Choir for the Nations.

Ian is a true pioneer of both Christian music media and cross-cultural music ministry!

—Nancy Honeytree-Miller
Honeytree/Windsong Ministries Inc.
Fort Wayne, IN

PROLOGUE

It's been there for as long as I can remember. I wanted to be a performer. As a young boy full of emotion, chutzpah, plus the semblance of talent, I wanted to be an artist and achieve. There has been and continues to be a stirring deep within my soul. My very spirit longs to sing, to soar, and to accomplish! I wanted to be a singer, musician, composer, actor, and producer. I longed to see my name on the marquee: William Ian Walker— Soloist, Choral Conductor, Producer, Director, Actor, Writer, Author. I dreamed of doing it all!

I have heard that artists can take many years to understand their elusive talent. As for me, my question is: "Why have I been given this talent and ability? Why do I have to overcome so much to become successful? How do I not let others abuse it?" Now into my fifties, I finally understand my role. It is to share my story.

As a serious twelve-year-old, I needed an escape from the many hours, days, and weeks of emotional sadness and constant verbal harassment that came because I was different. Being artistic and having a sensitive nature, I didn't fit in! I honestly did not know who I was or who I could be. "Consider Yourself One of Us," a particular show tune from the film *Oliver*, was quite significant to me. The many camera angles in the film portrayed life from varied spheres of wealth, sadness, and poverty. This scene left a lasting impression. My mind couldn't solely focus on the storyline per se, but I was very intrigued by its production, presentation, and portrayal.

Later in life, I would experience being in a movie and what being an "extra" was like. As a child, I allowed my mind to wander to capture moments of peace and to dream of the future. Walking home, I desperately tried to deny my emotional sadness. It was then that I reflected on these and other images from films.

My blessed grandma, Violet, was a powerful support to me through our many hours of tea-time sessions or while jointly polishing her silver tea service. She gave me her love and wisdom and her undivided attention. Grandma reassured me that I was in a normal "awkward stage" of my teen years. She said that things would start to get better once I was sixteen. I believed and trusted her. I shared with Grandma my artistic soul, my discoveries, and my aspirations; however, "the awkward stage" continued into my twenties, thirties, and early forties!

In those awkward years, I walked two miles coming home. Daily I had a paper route after school, which continued for all four seasons. I would imagine that a camera crew was filming me singing a new song. Living a fantasy life helped me cope. It was an all-consuming pastime.

Twenty years later I walked that familiar path back to my parents' home. Now as a man, I realized that I had lived in this dream-like state for many years. It became a comfortable release to escape the pain. Then the reality of life set in during my forties. At times, life is rough and cruel! I learned that God, my family, and devoted friends would help me navigate safely through my darkest, deepest valleys.

I would not be officially diagnosed with ADHD until the mid-1990s, ending many years of personal speculation. Medication helped to alleviate the emotional stress for a while, and therapy uncovered painful wounds and scabbed-over scars. For many years, these emotional wounds lay locked in the closet of my soul. *Why did all of this ugliness have to happen to me?* At the end of three long years of chaos, I finally began to receive hope, answers, and insight. Peace was a result.

Creative longings and dreams of being successful were as real to me as the colour of my hair and eyes. Medication helped balance some of my bursts of creative energy, and my demeanor would soften. This bandage approach proved to be temporary.

My secret of leaving many ADHD symptoms behind lies in God's perfect timing. With God's help, I have spent my life and career studying and developing my craft in the performing arts and in varied interests. The results are good, and I've proven to myself that I am capable. I have produced concerts, performed in plays, participated in my many vocal recitals, and conducted and produced choral music.

Stirring ... My Soul ... to Sing ... is my theme. At the end of the book, I have included a special section: Creative Impressions. These reflective ideas are at the end of most chapters; here you have an opportunity to reflect or journal your own stepping stones of growth.

My story is not a simple "how to overcome ADHD" story. ADHD, by its very nature, is complicated; however, the compensating attributes stemming from my passion for faith, music, and the arts (as well as a thirst for ongoing learning) helped me to stay positive. My memoirs are about hope, faith, and healing in God. I know that I could not have reached these mountain top experiences without my Heavenly Father.

Come with me as I reveal the wonderful testimony of God's plan for my life. I have learned so much, and I'm finally able to speak openly about heart and soul issues. My prayer is that my first-hand experiences will be a blessing and provide hope to you and yours. Let me encourage you to seek personal healing. Let the Holy Spirit's presence arise as you attain the loving vision that God has in His heart for you.

Performing at Parkside High School in 1977 (ECG Photo)

CHAPTER ONE
CAST, CHARACTER, AND CONNECTIONS

I was born, weighed, and named William Ian Walker. As with nearly a third of all human births, I was born with the umbilical cord around my neck. Most babies born in this state are unharmed and nothing is amiss. The doctors used their skills and knowledge, removing the tightly wrapped cord from my neck. From that momentary life-altering experience, I suffered some slight brain damage. The diagnosis later was Attention Deficit Hyperactivity Disorder, or ADHD, but I was born with another condition. Maybe you've never heard of it, but nevertheless, I was born with a song in my soul.

Without a doubt, I was created to serve the body of Christ and to build His kingdom. My dramatic entrance onto the stage of human life was only the beginning. I was not on that stage alone. As an ADD/ ADHD child, I will share with you more about my family trees. You will meet Charlie and Violet Helmkay, plus Edna and Alf Walker (my grandparents), plus my great aunts and uncles from both the Walker and Rashleigh Family.

THE UNFORGETTABLE CREW AND CAST OF CHARACTERS

As in any well produced drama, a significant line-up of strong cast and crew members would provide the support required for the script and score of my life. Before the curtain rises, please meet the crew.

Grandma Violet Helmkay-Garbutt: stage manager. I am told that our loving and doting grandma, Violet (Rashleigh) Helmkay-Garbutt, was looking after Mom and me as soon as we came home from the hospital. Grandma was the boss! She had that "knack" of creating a comfortable atmosphere for each new baby that was brought into the family. We were spoiled by Grandma's love and by her great homemade chocolate chip cookies. As Anne, my older sister, and I grew older, we helped Grandma in those early days of Mom's homecoming. With each new baby, Violet provided such a stable presence of love, joy, and fun.

As I grew in "stature" (I love that biblical reference), I had my grandma's loving and caressing arms. Don't get me wrong—my parents were also there for me with their love and support, yet Grandma knew how to let me be me! She was my advocate and cheerleader. Throughout my lifetime with Grandma, I expressed all my joys and emotional hurts to her. She blessed us all with her incredible faith. I am still emotional when I speak about my grandmother's deep love and affection for me.

My mother, Doreen (Helmkay) Walker: producer, director, nurturer, and leading lady. Doreen Walker was a "true woman of her time." In the early 1940s and 1950s, my mother followed God's purpose with His special "calling" on her life. She had an ability to cherish people and especially attend to the needs of pastors, teachers, and missionaries. My mother loved her husband, Bill, then her children, and later her eight grandchildren. My parents were married for fifty-six years and surrounded their children and grandchildren with a nurturing and loving Christian environment.

My mother, Doreen, and grandmother, Violet
(Walker Family Photo Collection)

Many friends and family have said to me: "You are so like your mother." Now that I am aging, I look like her as well. No other statement could make me feel so proud. I am honoured as others see the similarities in our personalities through Mom's passion for loving life, her compassion for others, her love of vocal and choral music, her outgoing personality, and her positive attitude. I couldn't have had a better role model to follow than my mom. I loved to watch Mom in her element, being inspired by the love of God.

Both my parents were raised with an abiding faith in God. They maintained their joint relationship to Jesus first, and then to each other. They nurtured their children and later grandchildren to develop their own personal walk of faith. Faith was also demonstrated in our household by godly and consistent discipline. As a strong couple, they were amazing role models in their joint passions, interests, marriage, and Christian legacy.

Doreen (Helmkay) Walker was never shy about speaking her mind. I, too, have inherited my mother's direct manner of communication. As I look at my genealogical background, I am amazed at the similarity between our two generations concerning our challenges with disability issues. Growing up in Toronto, Ontario, in the early 1930s, my mom left high school in Grade Eleven. As she obtained many jobs and gained valuable work experiences, Mom developed her own sense of style and independence. Later she instilled those same life skills in her children. In our teenage years, Mom and Dad both reminded us of how we should train ourselves to think outside of the box by being independent.

Doreen, my mom, loved to be involved in the Baptist Women Missionary Society (BWMS) and with other community projects. At the age of fourteen, she was a member of both her own church and her local BWMS chapter. She loved to sing and participate in choirs and had a passion for the classical choral standards and contemporary praise and worship music. Doreen became a mentor to many younger women. She worked diligently on many community projects, such as Meals on Wheels or the yearly World Day of Prayer. She loved to have fun, stimulate the conversation, organize and plan events, and welcome all ladies to grow deeper in their faith by reading, growing, and learning.

Mom loved music and excelled at it! She studied piano and voice as a young soprano soloist at the Toronto Royal Conservatory of Music (RCM). Her strong sight-reading skills opened many opportunities for her to sing solos and join in a large, city-wide choral ensemble known as The Toronto Baptist Choral Society. They performed Handel's *Messiah*, Haydn's *Creation* and the "passion play" entitled *The Triumph of Our Lord*, written by Toronto conductor and composer Arthur Pointer (a professor of composition at the Royal Conservatory of Music, Toronto).

Mom had a deep respect for Mr. Pointer's compositions portraying the different passions of Christ, whether in cantata style or in musical drama. Mom would speak of her involvement in portraying various biblical characters. These musical events affirmed her personal walk with the Lord. Participating in the dramas and musicals was very emotional for her. As a background singer or chorus member acting out the story of Christ, she took her responsibilities very seriously.

In 1948, Mom participated in the newly formed Youth for Christ Choir and its Toronto crusades. These evangelistic meetings involved the young Billy Graham. Mom's face would light up as she shared with her children her memories of singing in the choir and being a part of the future Billy Graham Evangelistic Association (BGEA).

My mother and father would support the BGEA for the rest of their lives. In September of 2008, with the help and support of Lorna Dueck, Christian broadcaster and friend, Mom met with Billy Graham's grandson, William (known as "Will"). Mom glowed as she shared these memories with him.

Elaine, me, and Will Graham (grandson of Billy Graham)
in Toronto, 2008. (ECG Collection)

Is it any wonder that Mom gave me her love of vocal music and the choral arts? I asked her, "When you were pregnant with me, were you involved in choral singing and church solo singing?" Her answer was yes to both questions. These family experiences, for me, were instrumental in developing a passion to be actively performing and working within the choral arts.

We four (Anne, Ian, Janet, Andrew) Walker kids thrived in the arena of not being afraid to meet new people and interact. Our public and human relations training began by just watching my mother and grandmother circulate among people. Always dressed to the nines, with her hair perfectly coiffed and nails done just so, Mom was in her natural element as she carried out her church and social duties.

Celebrating Doreen's seventy-fifth birthday with me at an Opera Tea House (Walker Family Photo Collection)

Doreen met Bill Walker at one of these Baptist events in 1951. It all started at Camp Kwasind, a Baptist Camp near Bracebridge, Ontario. Anne Wilson, one of my mom's dearest friends, recently told me that after one-year of dating, my parents were at camp and Doreen said, "Bill kissed me!" Although Bill was very conservative, with Doreen, he was interested! He loved her passionately. They were married in October of 1954.

Both born in 1931, Doreen and Bill were children of the depression. They inherited the work ethic that a man had a duty in the workplace and a woman was to stay at home and nurture the family. However, my mother was not a true domestic and hated housework! Mom taught her children to do the chores around the house—vacuuming, dusting, washing the clothes, and ironing. She taught her two sons to cook when she was working full-time. In 1973, Mom fulfilled a passion of her own by going back to school as a mature student and studying to become an RNA (now known as RPN). Mom's determination was a notable example to me in following through with one's dreams and aspirations. I too went back to university in 1996, 2004, and in 2008 to complete my education.

After Mom retired from nursing, she loved continuously building her own relationships and networks with her retired nursing buddies. Mom loved to party! She would organize annual Christmas dinners and other events.

All the Walker children and grandchildren have inherited our parents' outgoing nature. They shared their zest for life, their love of the wilderness and camping, and their passion for being involved in the Lord's work. Mom and Dad believed in open communication within the family as well as in their church community. Now a large family of eighteen, Mom's imprint remains evident. When I asked her to edit the family sections in this book, she gave me her open and honest feedback. In fact, because of her critical input, I can share these family stories and events concerning all the Rashleigh, Helmkay, and Walker families.

Mom didn't always have a profound sense of humour, but she loved a good joke. She wasn't great at repartee, but with her down-home common sense, she could enjoy moments of laughter, with tears flowing from her eyes, and participation in family moments. Mom and I also shared this similar characteristic: we don't tell jokes very well, mostly because we forget the punch lines!

We siblings all share our parents' passion and love for being active, involved, and committed. As senior members of Dundas Baptist Church, Bill and Doreen were shining examples of their solid marriage and passion.

During September 2009, Mom was hospitalized for tests that revealed the initial stages of colon cancer. Due to this and other complications,

Doreen went home to be with the Lord on May 6, 2010, in her seventy-ninth year. My mom and I were very close. A few days before she passed away, she told us all how proud she was of her four kids and said: "I have been so proud and blessed to be your mother and will love you all into eternity, until we see each other again. You all know where I am going, and I know that I'll see all of you very soon. You all have accepted the Lord, and we'll all be together again as a family in Heaven." What better legacy, testimony, and memorial can a mother leave for her children than that found in this statement? As a family, we were overwhelmed by the large crowds who attended her funeral. My mom was a seed-sower in the lives of so many.

Doreen's imprint on my life has been vast! We would chat on the phone two or three times per week, especially when she was ill. Since the mid-1990s, Mom and I had a great and loving relationship. Ten years earlier we faced and dealt with the difficult issues between us. Mom was so proud of me for finishing my education and working and writing toward finishing this book. Mom was my cheerleader. I was blessed with a wonderful mother! I miss her presence, her wisdom, and our weekly chats and hugs! I know that it won't be too long until we will be reunited in Heaven.

My dad, "Bill" Walker: stage and technical director, scenic designer. In theatre, the behind-the-scenes construction of the scenery is critical to the success of any performance. In many ways, my dad served that role in our family. My father, William Alfred Walker Jr. ("William the Third"), was known as "Bill." Generally a shy and humble man, Dad was the third of four siblings: Charlotte, Jim, Bill, and Clara. He was also the second generation of a sheet metal working family in a company launched in 1948 by my grandfather, Alfred, known as "Alf."

Before Dad passed away, he told me about his own disabilities. Being left handed in the 1930s meant that he was forced to write using his right hand. The result was less than satisfactory, and his penmanship was always poor. He also had difficulty in school with reading and comprehension. Bill stuttered and it was thought he needed therapy. Held back in school twice due to his own academic challenges, he excelled in mathematics.

This success and sports gave him the boost he needed in self-confidence. Later he developed both drafting and business skills.

After completing his apprenticeship, he had to prove to his father, Alf, that he had the talents and the skills to run the business. Following my grandfather's death, my Uncle Jim and Dad ran the business. When Dad was in his early sixties, he bought out his brother's share of the business. For another twenty years, Dad operated Walker Sheet Metal & Roofing of Hamilton. The business has now passed on to my brother, Andrew.

My favourite picture of my dad singing in the choir!
(Walker Family Collection)

My dad was the textbook example of a hard-working Christian businessman. Bill taught his children true ethics in the workplace and in the home. My dad had a wonderful sense of humour and was a story teller in his own way. Dad and his twin sister, Clara, were born in September of 1931. Bill was the older one. He was considered a "real boy" growing up in the depression years in the new development of Westdale in Hamilton. Dad often retold his stories of boyhood memories. His adventures were filled with slingshots, shooting rats at the nearby garbage dump, and getting into mischief. We loved to hear about Dad's Tom Sawyer-like adventures, which often displeased his mother, Edna. Along with our cousins, we would discover that our grandma (Edna Bracken Walker) was a very dignified Edwardian woman. She had been a rural minister's daughter in Huntsville, Ontario, who became a school teacher in her twenties. Together my grandparents purchased their first home in the community of Westdale.

Dad loved to share his teenage stories. Dad and his friends would attend the Saturday afternoon movies at the Westdale Theatre. The price of admission was five cents. Sometimes the group of friends would crouch down on the floor between the first two rows in front of the movie screen. Undetected by the attendant, my dad and his friends would watch the movie again!

Dad's close friend, Bill Lawrence, became a well-loved broadcaster. He started his career as a local news anchor at CHCH TV and then CBC Toronto television as a gifted weatherman. Bill was also the original host and producer of CHCH's *Tiny Talent Time*. Later in his career, Bill would broadcast "live" in front of Hamilton's City Hall for the Boy Scouts Parade. Dad would walk with his troops and give a salute to the mayor and other dignitaries. Bill Lawrence always gave my dad a special "back at you" salute as his scout troop marched by.

Bill Walker found his own system for developing self-esteem and leadership through his twenty-five years in scouting. He became the head scout master for his Westdale troop, based at McNeil Memorial Baptist Church. In his bachelor years, he was involved with the spring clean-up crew of Camp Kwasind and later Camp Oneida. He was a volunteer at Camp Oneida for over forty years.

Similar in passion, skills, and energy to our grandpa, Alf, Dad would not consider retirement until after his eightieth birthday. Losing Mom in 2010 and then his twin sister, Clara, in 2011, depleted Dad's energy. He worked full-time until early June of 2012, when he developed pneumonia and required hospitalization for nearly three weeks. When other complications developed, Dad's physical body could take no more, and on July 4, 2012, he went to be with the Lord.

During Dad's weeks in the hospital, I would visit him often, and Dad shared with me some of these stories. Some stories I already knew and some were brand new. Within my own spirit, I knew that Dad's life was ending and these "heart-to- heart chats" would indeed be our last.

My relationship with my dad wasn't always close, but as he said, "We could always talk." He had the nicest smile and when he would wink at you, you knew he was pleased to welcome you into his company. During those three weeks, a close bond between us formed. God had answered my prayers that we could be close. Little did I know that when we would pray together, Dad was transferring both his birthright and his anointing to me. Dad told me that he loved me and was very proud of me and all my achievements.

As a family, we dealt with Dad's passing, visitation, and funeral service. We heard amazing stories and memories of how he had touched many lives. After Mom had passed away, Dad was overwhelmed by the cards and personal notes from folks all over the world expressing their condolences to him and sharing how Doreen had blessed so many people. Now it was our turn to hear comparable stories about Bill and the seeds he planted. One profound passion of Dad's was for young people to experience Christian summer camping.

We siblings stood at the casket of our father and all prayed together. Each grandchild placed a carnation in his casket. We four adults had our last goodbye. I reached for two sunflowers in a flower arrangement. I gave one to Andrew and said to him: "We are sons of the King, and it is only fitting that we would place these 'son flowers' for our dad." I placed my sunflower beside his head and gave my thanks to both Mom and Dad for all that they had done for me.

Two nights before Dad's totally unexpected death, all of us were together. It was evident that Dad was at genuine peace as he saw his kids together. When the meeting broke up, we each said our goodnight to him. I gave Dad a hug and said, "I will see you soon." Dad gave me that smile and wink.

My father had been in the sheet metal industry for over sixty years. His staff spoke to me about his dedication to the industry and said that he gave the very best customer service. One comment was, "Your dad was the most honest person I ever met. He had integrity in everything that he did." I desire that Dad's honesty and integrity will be a living part of my legacy.

I've now introduced you to my parents; however, for any true story line, there is a rich, godly legacy. This inheritance, as Shakespeare said, is "the spur of my intent to prick excellence" (*Macbeth*, 1.7.25). This part of the story that I know is where my DNA for ministry began.

The torch of utmost commitment of our Christian heritage to the Kingdom of Jesus Christ has been passed down to all of us. Both great-grandfathers on my dad's side were in ministry. It was from these two great-grandfathers that five generations followed the teachings and lifestyle of the Christian faith.

Bracken and Walker—Great-grandfathers in ministry. My great-grandfather, the Reverend William James Bracken (father of Edna), was a maverick. He loved to plant new churches. James was born and raised in the village of Newbury, which is just outside of London, Ontario.

Reverend James Bracken was ordained in 1889 and became a travelling evangelist. He planted Maitland Street Baptist Church in London and then came to Hamilton to start Wentworth Street Baptist Church. He was also called to the pastorate of East Flamborough, Westover, and Freelton, Ontario. In 1892, James felt the call to go out west to Morden, Manitoba, and then to Louisville, Kentucky to attend Southern Baptist Theological Seminary. Following his graduation, he came back to London and was called to a "three-point charge" in Binbrook, Caistor, and Tyneside, Ontario, which is about thirty miles south-east of Hamilton.

Within a few years, Reverend Bracken was called to Ferguson Avenue Church in Hamilton. The congregation increased so rapidly that they needed to purchase new property to build Hughson Street Baptist Church. After ten years, James again felt "the call" to move his family west to Alberta. Later he was called for the second time to Hamilton and to the Hughson Street Church, where he remained for another nine years. James and his family then moved to Huntsville, Ontario, where he pastored the Southampton church until his death in 1933. Great-grandpa Bracken had served faithfully for forty-four years in the Baptist Convention of Ontario and Quebec. James Bracken's life and ministry were highlighted in his obituary:

Throughout his long ministry, Brother Bracken enjoyed many tokens of divine favour. By his simple, earnest Christian life he endeared himself to all his ministerial brethren. His religion is not emotional but practical, pure and undefiled.

His obituary was published in a number of publications, including the *Canadian Baptist Magazine* and *The Hamilton Spectator.*

Great-grandfather Bracken married three times. His first wife, Annabelle, died in childbirth, leaving Arthur and Clara. His second wife, Rachel Sillcox, was my great-grandmother. Their daughter, Edna, was my grandmother. When Great-grandfather passed away, he was survived by his third wife, Annabell, and their daughter, Norma.

My Grandmother Edna had a brother, Edgar Lewis, whom she always called "Lou," and two step-sisters, Clara and Norma. Edna had a step-brother named Arthur, in B.C., and George, in Calgary.

My other great-grandfather, William Burnett Walker, was born on October 22, 1869, in Leadgate County, Durham, England. William's family came from Workington, a region known as the heart of the steel and sheet metal industry. When William, or "Will," came to Canada in his late teens, he worked in the western provinces with the First Nations people before settling in Hamilton for seventeen years.

William worked for Stelco, beginning the line of sheet metal workers in my family, and then "felt the call" to go into ministry in 1909, at thirty-eight years of age, with his wife, Charlotte (Goodwin) Walker. They were married in 1899 and had four children: Alfred, Rita, Walter, and Pearl, the youngest, who was born in 1913. William left the family behind with his in-laws (the Goodwin family farm in Ancaster) while he studied for two years at Moody Bible Institute in Chicago. He graduated in 1907.

When William died in August of 1969, he had been active for forty-three years in the Baptist ministry, serving in southern and Southwestern Ontario: Bothwell, Kinmount, Oro, New Sarum, Innerkip, Selkirk, Chesley, Lakefield (for thirteen years from 1931–1944), and Springford. He retired in 1951.

William and Charlotte lived and retired in Lakefield from 1951–1965. Great-grandpa was six weeks short of turning one hundred when he died in August of 1969. William and Charlotte would have celebrated their seventieth wedding anniversary in November of that year. Charlotte died in 1973 at the age of ninety-seven.

In 2003, I filmed a video interview with my Great-Aunt Pearl and Uncle Walter. They'd both lived in Lakefield, Ontario all their lives. I asked them about their memories of their parents and what they remembered of their father's temperament. Both Uncle Walter and Aunt Pearl remembered being publicly chastised from the pulpit!

As a young man, William had a difficult life on his own in this strange land. As an Edwardian man and provider, William was in total control of his household, his family, and his ministry. He was very punctual, and if you were late, you would receive a lecture for your tardiness.

Sunset at the Walker cottage, one of the most glorious spots in the Kawartha Lakes (Walker Family Photo Collection)

LIFE AND TIMES AT THE WALKER COTTAGE
Reverend William and Charlotte Walker were given a choice piece of land in the Kawartha Lakes of Ontario. The donor was a farmer and congregation member who had many acres of prime land around the lake. He offered William (his pastor) the best piece of property.

William was also offered reclaimed wood from an old barn. This wood provided the material that was to become "the great-grandparents' cottage." In the late 1930s, the first "cottage" was a large, one-room cabin. In 1948, Alf built the second cottage. In 1950, a boathouse was added. Now four buildings are part of "cottage life" on this cherished property.

For me, the Walker family cottage has memories filled with emotions. In reflection, I now understand the symptoms of my ADHD. Some of my memories detailed fearful experiences of duties that were expected of me and how I should fulfill my manly place in the family. Rest, relaxation, and exercise are vital! In 2005, I wrote this journal:

"As a young boy, I can remember visiting my grandparents' cottage. After breakfast, Grandma would point out to me the nature-filled moments of life. Often she was at her portable sink (an oval, metal dish pan), heating the water with her old trusty kettle and finishing her dishes. Having arrived at the cottage and settled in around 1:00 a.m., our sleep was rudely interrupted by Grandpa's "noisy puttering" early the next morning, with him looking for something in the back shed You would have no choice and would need to get up. Grandpa and I never saw eye to eye nor was I one of his favourites. Often, we two grandsons were involuntary recruited as helpers. Grandpa had many chores in maintenance. There were many repairs to be done around the beach front area (e.g. replacing, enforcing, and rebuilding the stone embankment). We "Walker men and ladies" would all work together during long weekends and even during my parents' vacation."

My childhood chore was to fill up the copper reservoirs with lake water, which was required for washing dishes or sponge bathing. These copper containers were attached to the old wood burning stoves in both houses. At that time, there was no running water and there was no bathroom— only our family outhouse.

Standing on the dock dipping my two buckets into the lake was nerve wracking. With my metal buckets filled with the water, I would trudge them back up over the hill and fill up the reservoirs. I needed to make sure that I did the job correctly and properly. If the job was not done correctly, I knew I would be verbally corrected by my father. When I had completed my job, Dad would come and inspect my work. With some fear and trepidation, I waited for my dad to say that the job was done to his satisfaction.

Many boats were moored to the docks for our use. From an early age, Dad tried to teach me how to tie boat knots properly. I tried to remember the patterns from year to year and would curse myself, getting so frustrated because I couldn't remember the proper pattern.

In my teen years, I loved to get up early in the morning and row in the family skiff across the lake. The skiff was built by Uncle Walter (Alf's only brother) in the late thirties. Out on the lake in the morning air, I developed my rowing muscles, which became a part of my own yearly cottage routine.

Sunday mornings would require full family attendance at Lakefield Baptist Church, including all who were visiting at the cottage and/or the Lakefield relatives. Being at Lakefield Baptist was a delight! I sat with my grandparents and the rest of the family. As the singer and musician in the family, I love to sing solos at our summer church home. The wooden acoustics in the sanctuary are the best! I love singing in this church, as it was the last charge of Great-grandpa Walker's ministry.

UNCLE WALTER & AUNT PEARL—THE LAST OF THE ORIGINAL WALKER FAMILY UNIT

My Great-Uncle Walter and Aunt Pearl had a significant impact on my life. Both recognized my disability and they readily accepted me for my strengths. Both of my Walker grandparents passed away in the early 1980s and 1990s. The Walker family reunion now consists of forty-five to fifty people when we are all together.

Walter passed away at almost 102 years of age in October of 2009, and Pearl in March of 2012 in her ninety-ninth year. These two siblings were blessed abundantly with the good health and great longevity of the Walker genes.

Uncle Walter's constant devotion to his faith, and his long life, may be attributed to a very active and enjoyable career, as he was known as a "Master Canoe Builder." Secondly, he was a servant, elder, and deacon in the Lakefield Baptist Church for over seventy-five years. From his obituary, these words were written about his amazing life:

Walter was a faithful and active member of Lakefield Baptist Church for over seventy-five years, many of which he spent as Sunday School Superintendent and Deacon. Walter moved to Lakefield in 1931, where he began his boat-building career. He worked for several canoe companies in Lakefield and Peterborough. Through the years, he received several recognitions for his outstanding contributions to the art of canoe building. He was the first inductee as Canoe Builder Emeritus to the Canadian Canoe Museum, Peterborough. In 2003, he was inducted into the Stairway of Excellence at Galt Collegiate Institute, Cambridge, Ontario.

Uncle Walter, a very humble man, was a man of few words. Yet when he did speak to you, there was always love and respect. Family members would want to update Walter on one's recent boating or fishing experiences. Walter was an excellent craftsman. As the years went on in our relationship, he came to understand me and my artistic flair, love, and passion for life. Like him, Walter knew that my heart was to be a servant. At Walter's and Pearl's funerals, I was so honoured that both families requested that I sing.

Pearl (Walker) Hendren was an RN who worked for many years in the health system of Lakefield, Peterborough, and other surrounding clinics. Whenever someone needed medical services, Pearl was usually there. She was a generous giver and made a significant contribution to BWMS groups in her church. She was frequently the co-leader of many Christian projects within the Lakefield/Peterborough community.

Aunt Pearl and I were both April babies, and near our birthdays we would connect on the phone. With the passing of Pearl in March of 2012, the dynasty of the Walker family is now gone; however, the next generation is very active. Along with my second cousins, we all enjoy spending time with our Walker and Bracken relatives.

Wow, what awesome family genes I have been blessed with! Many have commented to me how blessed I am to have come from such a solid Christian heritage, and I couldn't agree with them more!

CHAPTER TWO
STAINED GLASS WINDOWS

Like most people, I don't remember much about my years as a toddler. Now that our immediate family is seventeen members strong, sometimes we talk about the 35mm slides documenting our experiences and memories. We recall the childhood places, events, and people that influenced us. Our parents provided many circles among all their close friends, camp and church friends, as well as during family vacations all over North America.

The last time I saw the slide show, I remember looking at photos of me taken during those impressionable years. From ages four through eight the expression is clear: there is evident sadness, and at times anger, on my face. I am told that I was not always a happy baby. Sometimes I was known as a moody child. As a young child, if I did not want to have my picture taken, I would totally disrupt the family event or storm off and have a temper tantrum.

Apparently, it was due to my short attention span or temperament that I always needed some type of moment-by-moment stimulation or entertainment. I enjoyed playing with Tinker Toys. I recall images of sticks and red building cubes as being fun for me. The simple toys would have interested me ... at least for a few minutes or so.

I am not always comfortable using mechanical tools. Instead, God gave me many artistic gifts, including the love of reading, learning, and writing—combined with passion for the performing arts and the love of language. Included in that package was an appreciation for the artistry of stained glass windows.

Stained glass windows fascinate me to this day! I can look at these windows and works of art for hours. Perhaps it's the artwork, the shapes and forms within the design, that interests me. I think my love for stained glass art started when I was in first grade in public school. Sitting in church, I would look and marvel at the McNeil Memorial Baptist Church windows, our first church home in Hamilton.

Mrs. Miniver is a classic film, set during the Second World War. At the end of the movie there is a wonderful scene involving stained glass. It takes place in the setting of a dome-like presence of a burned-out church building that has become an open-air altar of broken stained glass scattered throughout the sanctuary. The final scene of the film shows the family resuming their traditional practice of attending weekly Sunday morning services. There has been great loss in the community. Many church and family members were killed during the war. The family's heart, home, and church sanctuary have been devastated. The movie ends with the family and the community ready to embrace their new post-war beginnings. This new beginning brings both joys and sorrows. The Miniver family and the community are comforted by being in God's house. To me, McNeil Baptist Church represented that Sunday tradition of constantly gathering together as a family for worship.

Being a typical Baptist church, the beginning of the service would start with an "introit of the choir" proceeding into the sanctuary during the opening hymn. At the age of six, I enjoyed the swell of the organ, the congregation standing, and the ritual of the choir processional into the sanctuary. On truly bright, sunny days, the brilliant light from the stained-glass windows would fill the room with a heavenly presence. God was in His house!

Sitting with my father and Grandma and Grandpa Walker (who were founding members of the church), I would soon get bored and somewhat fidgety. From the choir loft, Mom would give me that special look to imply "stop fidgeting and behave." Dad would notice my disruptive nature and quietly have me sit beside him. He would pull out his trusty mechanical pencil and a pad and let me draw on the pad or church bulletin. One Christmas Eve service a few years back, I watched my brother, Andrew, employ this exact gesture with his children—doing the same thing that our Dad did when we were fidgeting. Both my father and my brother just let the child draw, thus reassuring them that church was a safe place, even when little children are bored.

If I was fidgety, Grandma Walker would give me either a peppermint or a Life Saver candy. To me, sucking on a candy and considering those wonderful stained-glass windows was such a treat on a Sunday morning. God was revealing Himself to me, even as a little child. From a small boy of around eight or nine years old, I felt deeply the presence of the Holy Spirit, right near me and gently speaking or leading me.

Even now when I am near beautiful stained glass, something inside of my spirit tells me that I am in touch with God, that should He speak to me I am ready to hear His voice. I would later learn how ADHD and its symptoms would prick my self-esteem for many years into the future. The peacefulness of watching the light shine rapidly on those stained glassed windows would bring peace to my emotionally charged mind, body, and spirit.

After the service was an entirely different story. I became a holy fireball. I could not stop running in and out of the church building. I am told that due to the cement steps leading up to the entrance of the sanctuary, I would usually tear a hole in my new gray flannel wool pants, requiring new pants to be purchased almost every week. Finally, my mother became wise to my ways and ironed two patches inside the knees of my pants, new or old.

Early on Sunday mornings, my dad would prepare his Sunday school lesson and we would have the TV on. We'd usually watch Kathryn Kuhlman's program, *I Believe in Miracles* (on CBS), and begin to prepare our hearts for the Sunday morning worship. As we'd watch, my spirit would gravitate to hers. In her weekly message or interviews of guests, Miss Kuhlman would focus on the presence of the Holy Spirit. Who knew that in my late twenties to my forties, Kathryn Kuhlman's messages and ministry, along with those of the Benny Hinn Ministry, would burn within me? I wanted to learn more about drinking, walking, and seeking the holiness of God.

Something extraordinary happened to me in May of 1966. I was blown by a freak fierce wind into a meshed wall of crushed stone. I remember being close to a creek embankment about two houses up from our then-home. As I recall, I was either on my bike or a friend's bike. The wind blew me hard against the meshed, crushed stone wall of a somewhat dried-up creek.

As I hit the wall, my body slammed up against the rock face. I had a deep cut just under my lip. Somehow, through God's grace or the intervention of an angel nearby, I could calmly get out of the creek and come home, crying that I needed medical attention right away! That cut required only three stitches, but the emotional scar would last longer than the physical scar.

In my thirties, I began to seek the Lord about the times in my life when "the spirit of fear" attempted to enter my body. He showed me the root cause of this visual, childhood incident and how even at the age of six, God was already working much deeper than anyone realized. At that very same time, the enemy (Satan) was trying to destroy me. The enemy tried to bring the elements of fear into my life; he even tried to steal God's joy that I was experiencing through new seedlings of my gifting and abilities.

As a lover of the light and in reading and studying the Word of God, I learned to develop and grow the seedlings of my gifting and abilities. I learned to equip myself with these talents in worship, prophecy, and the art of verbal and written communications. For me, walking with Jesus and being in His light begins my daily communications with God—especially, of course, when I'm around the brilliance of stained glass windows.

CHAPTER THREE
REAL-LIFE READ-THROUGHS AND DRESS REHEARSALS

I love the piano. Always have. I just didn't like learning how to play, read music, or practice. At age six, by ear I plucked out the tune of "Kumbaya" on the piano, and that was the beginning of piano lessons. God and my family genes have given me the gift of a good ear, and I loved hearing my teachers play my upcoming piano selections. The trouble was, I wasn't serious about learning musical phrasing at the piano by reading the notation on the page. I simply memorized and copied their hand movements.

For a long time, I could fake my progress, even without practicing. I had three different piano teachers in my youthful days. "Auntie Mo" was my first piano mentor. I know that I challenged Auntie Mo with my distinctive learning style. She instilled in me the beginnings of how to read music and interpret rhythm and phrasing at a very early age. My siblings and I didn't have far to walk to get to Moreen Thomas' home, or "Auntie Mo'," for our weekly music lessons.

Moreen and John Thomas were close friends of my parents from their initial courting days, and indirectly they encouraged our parents to become a couple at Camp Kwasind in the early 1950s. When our family moved to Dundas, Ontario in 1967, on the recommendation of my mother, the Thomas family bought a piece of property just down the hill from us. Who would have known that their sons, Dave and Ian Thomas (for whom I am named), would become Canadian icons in both pop music and improvisational comedy through Dave's association with SCTV?

With Dave and Ian Thomas, celebrating Dave's honorary doctorate from McMaster University in 2010 (ECG Collection)

Recently when Ian Thomas and I were together, we met with Mo's new friend. Thomas, who has incredible wit and a passion for drama and language, commented, "I'm so honoured to meet you. You are surrounded by a pair of Ian bookends." That was a humorous moment. Since 2004, I have reconnected with Auntie Mo. Now in her early nineties, Mo still has a wonderful command of the piano.

My renewed relationship with Mo has also been helpful to me as a singer and musician. Now the tables are somewhat turned. We have performed together in churches or at her home Christmas parties, with me being either the soloist or conductor, while Mo has been my accompanist. She has also been a guest lecturer to my youth choir.

I am pleased to say that the student has learned from his teacher. With respect to performance, including preparation for music exams or vocal recitals, one of the best "words of wisdom" was imparted to me by Auntie Mo: "Work hard on your musical notation and interpretation," she said. "That's learning your craft. Once you're confident and feel ready to perform, on the day of the performance, relax, breathe, and have fun with the experience." Those words continue to guide me each time I perform.

I wish the same sense of enjoyment could have guided me during my childhood piano practice sessions, but that isn't what I recall. Mom had a good ear and could tell when my timing was off, or if I missed a note in the piece that I was attempting to learn. Once while I was practicing at around age eleven, Mom critiqued my playing while she was ironing right next to me: "You missed that note" and "Your timing is all wrong. Do it again!" That was quite enough of her back-seat critiquing. I slammed my fingers on the piano keys and shut the piano cover, vowing never to play again. We got into an argument, but realizing she had a hot iron in her hand, I decided to give in and work on the difficult selections of the musical piece rather than be branded for life. Had my mother not been so insistent about the proper way to rehearse and dissect a piece of music, I may not have developed my own "musical ear" for dissecting one's technical performance.

Once I became an adult and started to pay my own way for piano lessons, that all changed. It took me a while to learn to read music in four-part harmony. I was in my late teens when I finally developed this skill. When I took up the accordion, I needed to learn how to read the bass clef. I love teaching, voice training, and perfecting each phrase or vocal piece. I teach my students how to develop their own ear through vocal training, production, and nurturing of the singer within.

While Auntie Mo and my mom were significant early musical influences on my young life, they were not the only influences. I still remember seeing *Mary Poppins*, my very first Disney movie, at the age of six. What an experience! It made a huge impression on me. I still recall the theatre itself, with the cut-out promotional figures of Mary Poppins hanging from the ceiling, the popcorn, and the concession stand—it seemed magical. In the 1960s, when a film was about to begin, heavy red curtains slid open, and when it ended, the curtains shut again. This Disney film became firmly rooted in my memory. I watched in awe as the animated film effects sprang to life in this incredible family film.

Julie Andrew's soprano voice was one of the first classical or theatrical voices I ever heard, and I was enchanted. Her British accent was an element of my daily experience in my own family; it flowed easily for me through the gift of my "ear," and it embraced me with a sense of familiarity and comfort. Though it's been more than fifty years since this film premiered, the movie captivated me to the degree that I still know the lyrics to most of the songs. I simply had to have the album (and now of course the DVD) and some of the other toys from the movie. I'm told that when I played outside with my young friends, I sang "A Spoonful of Sugar" while carrying an open umbrella—just like Mary Poppins, dancing up and down the street of our old Hamilton homestead. That was it! I was forever bitten by the "bug" of the dramatic entertainer.

My dear friend, international soprano and Canadian diva Adrianne Pieczonka, shares a similar experience with Andrew's performance style. She also remembers Julie Andrews in *Mary Poppins* becoming her first professional-voice role model. How many others were inspired to pursue musical theatre because of that film? Countless, no doubt.

In my first year of elementary school, I was asked to conduct a band of Carl Orff instruments with blocks, triangles, and wooden sticks in a rendition of "The Stars and Stripes Forever," the famous Souza march. The event was a 1967 celebration of Canada's Centennial during our special public school pageant, and I took it seriously. Using a wooden baton and conducting a 2/4 beat pattern that made my parents proud, I led my grade one class in the public performance—a memorable and positive debut for a young performer. I received my first standing ovation! Not bad for a kid air conducting his first professional gig!

In the early 1970s, our family listened to The Guess Who, The Beatles, Carole King, John Denver, Billy Joel, Elton John, and, of course, The

Partridge Family. I had a huge crush on Shirley Jones! When I was in my early teens, I attended my first classical piano concert. I knew in advance it would be a Liberace concert at Hamilton Place. Theo Howett, a dear lady in our church, invited me as her guest. She and I had a wonderful relationship, and I called her Grandma Theo. She loved Liberace!

By this time, I'd been studying piano for four to five years, but I'd never watched an artist and showman like Liberace, nor could I conceptualize that any serious classical artist would conduct themselves or their career in this manner. Mesmerized with his diamond rings, exotic costumes, and props, I absorbed every moment of his magical show. I could never have guessed that in 1978, working as a doorman at Hamilton Place, I would have another opportunity to meet him myself and get his autograph.

This wasn't my first piano concert. As a family, we had attended many community concerts. When Hamilton Place first opened in the mid-1970s, we attended various concerts and genres of orchestral, opera, and even dance concerts in the christening of this new hall. At that time, Boris Brott was the artistic director of the Hamilton Philharmonic Orchestra (HPO). He is now recognized as an international conductor, performing in many established concert venues.

Brott's name was regularly mentioned in our home, as the three oldest of us children had been to many of his children's concerts sponsored by the Hamilton Board of Education. Brott's concerts were always interesting, educational, and entertaining. They taught us much about music—from classical to pop—and about orchestral instruments and their environment, function, and impact, and about musical "colour" that shapes the dynamics of an orchestra.

I learned so much from Brott's concerts that when I worked for Orchestra London Canada in the 1980s, I felt very much at home. Brott continues to be involved with music education. He is constantly encouraging and equipping the next generation of artists/audience and patrons alike to participate in and sponsor various arts programs. During those student days, I read everything I could on Brott's career, with an interest in his innovative programming and development ideas for better cross-pollination of business with the arts.

Singing has also played a prominent role in my life. For me, singing has always been pure enjoyment. But what I wouldn't know until later into my musical studies would be how singing and choral training would be such a blessing to me with my ADD/ADHD tendencies, and how it would give me such a purpose of destiny and self-sufficiency.

From ages six to ten, my sister Anne and I sang with the Mennonite Children's Choir of West Hamilton. We had a talented German conductor, Madelyn Enns, who had an incredible way with children. Miss Enns was a tough cookie. No fooling around in her choir! We tackled some difficult choral pieces within the Canadian repertoire, which included various international folk songs. Many of these selections are still vivid in my memory.

At the age of nine, and still very much a boy soprano, I began my vocal training with Joanne Hansen. I studied with her for four years until my voice changed at thirteen. Mrs. Hansen's strength was teaching her students how to breathe and develop good vocal technique. I still remember my first lesson. "I'm going to teach you to breathe from your diaphragm," said Joanne, picking up a hardcover book. "Lie down on the floor." I lay down on the floor as I was asked. My assignment was to practice lifting the book off my stomach with my diaphragm muscles. "Practice this exercise fifteen to twenty minutes a day," she said. Demonstrating another technique, Joanne took a deep breath to tighten her stomach muscles, and then she asked me to place one hand on her stomach and the other hand in the same location on her lower back area.

She exhaled slowly, making a "hissing sound" until all the air from her stomach was gone and she needed to take a breath. Through this exercise of learning to breathe properly from the diaphragm, Joanne showed me how to "tank back up again," and gradually how to hold the quality of one's breath. For a boy of nine, the experience was unnerving—both scary and exhilarating. I travelled thirty miles from Dundas to East Hamilton on a city bus for lessons with Joanne. With this new independence came the discipline of having to be on time for Saturday morning lessons. Today I use both of Joanne's techniques in working with all my new students and choir members from the very first day of their vocal training.

My weekly voice lessons continued until involuntarily, but naturally, my voice changed. I observed and learned from my teacher, from my mother, and others who were accomplished singers. One memory of my mother comes to mind of how as a seasoned singer, she expertly handled an awkward situation.

A trained church soloist, my mom was very much in demand. One Sunday Mom was singing a solo piece and lost her place in the music. Instead of carrying on with the performance, she stopped the accompanist and asked her to start over. Even as a young singer I knew that wasn't a common thing to do. Mom made a choice that gave her control over her performance. As a result, she delivered the piece with command and passion. It was the bravest example I have seen of a singer taking charge over a situation that could have been a vocal train wreck. Rather than giving a mediocre performance, my mother took a risk and carried on as if nothing had happened.

BUILDING MY OWN MUSICAL AND MINISTRY IMPRINT

By 1973, my boy-soprano days were over and there were no more high "C's" for me. During the next three years, while my voice was changing, I couldn't keep up my vocal technique. I was advised not to put too much pressure on my changing singing voice, and I had dreams of wanting to become a tenor, as tenors are always in demand. By 1976, however, my voice settled as a bass/baritone, but during this time it cracked at the most inopportune moments.

Just like Peter on the *Brady Brunch* television series, my voice broke at the most embarrassing times when it was changing. At thirteen, I began studying the accordion, and in five years earned my Grade Five level through the Ontario Conservatory of Music. I initially studied with Beth McBain and the legendary Silvio Camilleri, a Hamilton and Golden Horseshoe accordion master, versatile musician, producer, and director with his own accordion orchestra. From Silvio, I learned about being successful as a teacher and director in your own local musical community.

I also learned how to dream, plan, and grow my individual musical vision. Silvio's vision influenced many youth and adults into continuing music education. I had always dreamed of achieving a bachelor's degree through an Ontario university music program. The accordion to me just didn't have enough academic cachet for continuing full-time studies, so the accordion was not the right instrument to pursue. I began diligently working on my voice, piano, and theory rudiments through the RCM credential program. I aspired to become a full-time voice and music major.

Again, ADHD challenged me. This is when ADHD symptoms became evident and a challenge in my life. Completing my public and high school years were difficult enough. My dreams and goals of taking a university music program had to be delayed until I could be admitted as a mature student.

As a member of a family of faith, I always loved Sunday school, especially when we would learn about missionaries from other lands. Being a visual learner, I loved seeing the slides of these international projects that our small tithes and offerings were supporting. Starting at ten cents and then advancing later to twenty-five cents, we were taught to give a portion of our weekly allowance. We were to personally support these projects overseas as well as be faithful in our prayer support. There would be special songs to sing, perhaps in other languages, that were a part of the entire mission band experience.

My parents had a deep and personal walk with God. They believed that God would provide for their daily and weekly provisions. Mom and Dad had such a passion for serving and being a support for overseas missionaries. When they were first married, they began supervising two "mission homes" in the Hamilton area. In some instances, we developed mutual interests or relationships with these folks and their children. My parents sought God if they should support these missionaries' efforts prayerfully or financially.

We often had missionary families as guests at home for one of Mom's home-cooked meals; many of these folks served in Bolivia, throughout South America, and in India. Sometimes these missionaries, knowing that we were a musical family, would bring their native instruments and would play for us. Many of these initial missionary contacts have passed on; however, their children remain in contact with me and my siblings.

Due to the seeds of my great-grandfathers' passion for faith on both the Bracken and Walker sides of the family, this commitment to serve God's family of servants has continued down to me and to my nieces and nephews (the fifth generation).

The summer of 1977 was a very significant summer for me. I was seventeen, and for five weeks I served as a Baptist Youth Corps worker at First Baptist Church, Meaford, Ontario—one of the most glorious tourist spots in Georgian Bay. I worked with youth as an interim missionary/pastoral summer student, using my musical gifts and assisting with other duties as required. At the time I didn't know it, but in the sanctuary of this church I was about to have yet another encounter with God that would redirect my life. In that sanctuary, God spoke audibly to me and transformed my life into that of a committed believer, worshipper, and future artist.

One morning while leading worship with my accordion in the sanctuary, I heard someone calling my name during the service three times. The first time I looked around the room to see who was calling me. It was a male voice, but I couldn't see anyone. I thought that it was one of the elders of the congregation who was very involved in the choir. I looked at him, but it wasn't his voice that had spoken to me, yet the message resounded clearly three times: "Ian ... worship me." God had audibly called my name! (see 1 Samuel 3:8)

I had been walking as a committed believer for four years since I was thirteen but had never experienced such an encounter. I am reminded of the biblical story of Samuel, whom God also called by name three times. When I realized God was talking to me, I was stunned! God, or the Holy Spirit, spoke until He got my attention. I was in shock for a few days after this encounter, and the only person with whom I could share this personal, supernatural experience was someone I knew I could trust—Grandma Violet.

Grandma knew that I had been given a special "connection with God in worship." She had prayed with me to develop it, especially when we began to work together as soloist and accompanist. I remember when I shared with her this experience, Grandma had tears in her eyes and told me, "Ian, you are destined for wonderful things; pray and ask God for more direction about these matters. When you are able, tell your parents about this experience."

I decided that I needed to mature first, and I knew they needed to see for themselves how I was influenced passionately when I either sang solos or was involved in praise and worship.

The words "worship me" burn in my heart even today. It has taken until recently for me to understand what the Holy Spirit was asking of me. Since the year 2000, I have gained a better understanding of these words and how that visitation would impact my life!

I love the scriptural reference that tells us that Mary pondered all of the things Gabriel shared with her in her heart (Luke 2:19). Oh boy! Can I ever relate to that visual image! Why God chose that very moment to speak into my life is still a mystery to me. This encounter certainly let me know of the Father's personal love and passion for me. He knew the deep challenges that I was yet to face in finishing public high school and even university.

During the five weeks of this youth ministry experience, I was paid some salary and moved around each week. To get a better perspective of their community and what rural life was like, I lived with five different families. The Meaford Church family became my extended family and a place where I could grow musically, support the local church, and gain valuable leadership skills.

The Meaford experience allowed me to stay in touch with my Great-Aunt Olive and Uncle Charlie Knight. Spending time with them for a week or so formed a lasting relationship between us and our two families. I will go into greater detail about my Aunt Olive and her family in a later chapter.

BEING A "DOORMAN" AT HAMILTON PLACE

In August of 1977, I volunteered to be a host at our church convention. The National Baptist Federation Assembly was held at Hamilton Place. This was my first opportunity to have access to the backstage elements of this theatre and arts complex. In Grade Ten, I applied for a part-time job at Hamilton Place and was hired as a doorman. My job was to rip tickets, escort disabled or regular patrons to their seats, and/or act as a security guard when called to do so.

This part-time job offered some exciting "perks." At the end of a show, if we (ushers or doormen) were around the stage door area, we could meet the artists, musicians, and celebrities that would leave through the stage door of the theatre. I met and received autographs from Harry Belafonte, Janis Ian (I thought that it was strange that anyone would choose Ian as a last name), Liberace (he loved performing at Hamilton Place), and Gordon Lightfoot.

One time, one of Gordon Lightfoot's aides indicated he needed me for something. It was the end of the show, and as I approached Mr. Lightfoot's dressing room, I saw at least sixty cases of beer stacked up against the walls. I had a copy of the concert program in my pocket, and once his aide had made his request of me, I pulled out my program and asked Mr. Lightfoot if I could have his autograph. It was obvious that Gordon was feeling no pain that evening.

As a doorman, I would occasionally be asked to fulfill some other duties that were not in our job description. The National Ballet of Canada would perform on tour at the theatre, and they would need background people to fill in at contrasting times of the ballet. We were asked to fill in as "townsfolk" for one or two times during their Hamilton performances. There I was dressed in one of these costumes on stage, tights and all, at Hamilton Place, blending in with other county folk on stage, and I was placed centre stage and enjoyed every minute of it!

I am always amazed when moments or fragments of my creative life come full circle. On June 8, 2009, at my McMaster University convocation—again at Hamilton Place—I thought about these fun-filled activities and the celebrities I met while working as a doorman. Bruce Cockburn, Canadian and international folk artist and humanitarian, received an Honorary Doctorate and was our featured speaker at the event. As I was coming forward to receive my diploma, I realized this would be my second appearance on stage at Hamilton Place. Before receiving my diploma and having a memorable hooding experience from Dr. Red

Wilson, Chancellor of the university, I chuckled to myself as I thought about my ballet debut.

My part-time job at Hamilton Place meant I could not always get my homework done. In Grade Eleven, my sliding grades meant I had to give up the position. I wasn't asked back as a doorman the next year because I "mingled too much with the artists." Twenty years into the future, my Hamilton Place experience was the catalyst that developed my strong appreciation and ability to be very comfortable meeting and socializing with many international artists.

OUR HIGH SCHOOL MUSIC DEPARTMENT: SINGER, CONDUCTOR, AND PRODUCER

Having studied piano and accordion, I wanted to play a lighter instrument that wouldn't be too difficult to carry. I chose the flute, and it didn't take too long for me to develop a good embouchure. Once I was good enough, my parents bought me a flute of my own. Parkside High School's music department was very well known in the community, and some of Hamilton's Philharmonic Orchestra alumni were recruited from our music department.

One Parkside alumnus, John Fanning, C.M., musician and singer, has gone on to international fame and has recently been given the Order of Canada. John has been a regular vocal artist at the Metropolitan Opera and has performed all over the world for many years, including engagements with the Canadian Opera Company. John and his family have been close family friends and members of Dundas Baptist Church, where I grew up.

During our Grade Ten music class, we had the original members of The Canadian Brass (then part of the Hamilton Philharmonic Orchestra) visit our music department. They presented a master class and insight into careers in music. This event was one of those pivotal moments during my high school music education. When the Canadian Brass became world famous, I was able to secure the autographs of the original members of the ensemble on one of their popular albums, and it's in my personal collection.

*"The Gang of Four" barbershop quartet from 1977–1980
at Parkside High School (ECG Collection)*

As all this ongoing music-making and studying was going on during my teenage years, Michael Rutledge (my long time high school chum and fellow musician) and I became interested in barbershop singing. We wanted to form our own group, which we called "The Gang of Four." Michael M., former child actor who had performed on many stages of North America and Europe, became our tenor, Michael Rutledge was lead, Frank De Clara was baritone, and I was bass.

We needed a teacher's supervision so we asked Mr. Dan Stevens, our current music teacher, to take us on. Dan Stevens loved our barbershop group and was most supportive of our efforts. Developing a quartet takes time, and we would be huddled around the piano, note bashing and listening to our voices blending together. Our rehearsals would run an hour (three early mornings a week) before eight o'clock in the morning!

Dan Stevens had a music military background and was a perfectionist when it came to quality and precision in his bands. He loved to teach his students the elements of learning and appreciating good jazz and Broadway music. Jazz and Broadway music became regular staples in Stevens' programming, along with classical music. To this day, I have a heartfelt appreciation for jazz and rhythm and blues due to Mr. Stevens' method of teaching this genre of music to his students. It must have been our youthful energies and the excitement that we were doing something creative and exciting that motivated me for these rehearsals so early in the morning. Now I hate to sing or to start teaching before 9:00–10:00 a.m.

In our second year, we had another faculty member supervise our barbershop group. The late Grant Betzner was a science teacher; however, he was also an amazing musician in his own right. We learned much about blending our voices, hitting the right notes, and effective modulation under his direction. He was an outstanding keyboard and harpsichord player, and we all appreciated his musicality—right when we needed him!

We performed at school concerts, church functions, socials, or wherever we were asked to sing. For my fortieth birthday, Michael Rutledge put together some of the wonderful live performances of our barbershop years on one CD. I love to listen to our youthful sounds and remember the three years of fun that we had in assembling this quartet.

MY INITIAL CONDUCTING DEBUT—WHAT AN EXPERIENCE!

In the 1980s, during my senior high school years, I was interested in instrumental and choral conducting. I was thinking that I should learn all that I could about "conducting." Michael Rutledge (trumpet), Frank DeClara (French horn), Ted Blandford (tuba or baritone), and Megan Glass (trombone) were experimenting with the formation of their own brass quartet. I volunteered to be their conductor. Usually brass quartets don't require conductors and they work as an ensemble, asking the horn player to count them in. Being very bold and brassy (no pun intended), I wanted this conducting experience of working with these young musicians. We had the opportunity to perform in our annual music night at the school, and the brass ensemble was ready to perform.

I don't even remember the name of the piece that the quartet was playing. I had the conducting baton in hand, preparing for a difficult part in the music. However, I didn't have a solid grip of the baton and somewhere in the transitional part of the piece, my baton went flying into the air and landed on the ground with a ping! It broke up the musicians in the quartet with laughing. They did, however, manage to finish their performance. So much for my classical conducting debut! As I recall, with much chagrin, Mr. Stevens played the taped recording in our music class over and over. He carefully instructed the class to listen for the point when the baton went flying and all of the brass musicians broke up. How embarrassing! Even at my fiftieth birthday celebration, Ruth and David Lee, good friends of my parents for many years and excellent musicians in their own right, informed me that their family were all in attendance during my "brass conducting debut." Their family still remembers and refers to me as "the chap with the flying baton!"

LEAVING OUR MARK ON THE PARKSIDE HIGH MUSIC DEPARTMENT

In the early 1980s, Michael, Frank, and I wanted to leave something as our legacy to the music department with our very own Music Banquet Event, coordinated at the end of the school year in June. For years, our school had acknowledged all the sports teams with their awards and banquet. We musicians and artists felt left out and decided that with all the musical activities and talent going at full throttle throughout the year, we would create our own banquet and awards evening. Ordering the food was easy—we just called our local KFC outlet and bought pop beverages and sold tickets to cover our costs. With ten of us on the committee, we created distinct categories to be designated. I recall in the initial year of the banquet (which was a surprise to us), The Gang of Four won one of the awards. Our small committee provided a service to the artistically inclined, non-sports minded people through this banquet. It was an enormous success and the tradition continued well into the early 1990s. Who would know that from the small beginnings of involvement in organizing these projects would develop my full-time career as a professional fundraising and arts consultant—along with music making, of course? Today I am required to assist in the planning of many unique events.

INITIAL MILESTONES FOR CHORAL MUSIC

In 1979, Michael Rutledge and I decided to audition for a spring student choral experience with the Ontario Youth Choral and Instrumental

Program in London, Ontario. This choral experience was sponsored by Fanshawe College's continuing education program. We both applied and were accepted into the Youth Singers musical event.

Michael, a tenor, and I, a bass/baritone, were selected into this program for high school music students across Ontario. The program showcased both choral and instrumental music. We would receive the music ahead of time to review, perfect, and rehearse. This repertoire required an additional five-day rehearsal schedule, culminating with a live performance on the Sunday afternoon for both chorus and orchestra. Our hosts during my years of involvement in the program were Gerald Fagan, music coordinator, and Marlene Fagan, accompanist.

Michael and I met other teens from all over Ontario. We were billeted in and around the London area. Some of the singers became my life-long friends. At the age of nineteen, this event was my first ever semi-professional choral experience, where I had to be prepared mentally and vocally as a chorister.

I still have the LP recordings of the two live concerts we performed in 1979. I returned to the program again in 1980. During those two years in this singers' program, I decided to work towards being accepted into the University of Western Ontario's (UWO) Faculty of Music vocal program.

In 1978, a gifted young choral conductor, Robert Cooper, had just completed his master's in choral conducting at the UWO. He had been given a Canada Council grant to study in both Germany and in the USA under Helmut Rilling and the late Robert Shaw, of the Robert Shaw Chorale. Robert Cooper had just taken over as artistic director from Gerald Fagan, the founder of the Toronto Mendelssohn Youth Choir (TMYC).

In 1978, Robert Cooper, simply known as "Cooper," was appointed as the choir's artistic director by the Mendelssohn Choir office and interacted with Dr. Elmer Iseler, music director and conductor of the Toronto Mendelssohn Choir. In 1980, Cooper was invited as guest conductor to the Ontario Youth Singers.

A unique bond developed between Robert (Bob) Cooper and me. The friendship continued into a mentorship, now almost forty years later. My connection with Cooper continues in our shared love and a heartfelt interest for choral art and its administration. After the Youth Singers experience, Cooper invited me to audition for the TMYC experience.

My acceptance into this semi-professional youth choir in the fall of 1980 turned my entire world upside down! At twenty years old, I became a "senior member" (due to age, not choral experience) and participated from September 1980 until June of 1982. Once the year's rehearsal schedule was set, TMYC events took priority in my life—next to my church and youth group activities. I was extremely committed to this youth choir. I traveled by GO bus weekly to rehearsals from Hamilton into Toronto.

Cooper said I was a late bloomer—so true in several respects. Even in getting my driver's license at nineteen, rather than at sixteen, I took my time in these matters. At the end of my first year in the choir, I obtained my license. During my second year in TMYC—and using the family car—I commuted approximately an hour's drive away from home into the big city of Toronto for rehearsals.

Under Robert Cooper's leadership, TMYC achieved a high standard of choral excellence, and we had great fun and fellowship at the same time. Each fall he took all eighty-plus of us on a retreat to Bolton, Ontario, for a musical weekend to get a head start with Christmas music preparations.

I cherish these memories and the choral singing performance opportunities during these impressionable years. Even today I still retain some of the great friendships and professional contacts that began during those formative years. From my experience with TMYC in 1981, I prepared for acceptance into university and focused my energies toward a career either as a professional music educator or as an arts administrator.

For twenty-three years Robert Cooper was the heart, soul, and passion of the Toronto Mendelssohn Youth Choir until the end of his tenure in 2001. Sadly, the choir is no more as of 2009. "Cooper" is very devoted to his "TMYC alumni" and to the well-being and development of his choristers. He remains respected and honoured as one of Canada's national and international choral treasures. In June 2003, Robert Cooper, C.M. received an honorary doctorate from Brock University for his significant contribution to the Canadian choral community, and in October 2003, he was appointed to the Order of Canada for his national contribution to choral music and his devotion to music education.

As of 2001, more than three thousand young people have participated as members of the TMYC association. Many of Canada's up-and-coming vocal artists now performing on the concert stages and opera houses around the world are alumni of TMYC. The international and Canadian superstar tenor, Michael Schade, was a "diamond in the rough" during his performance training years with the youth choir.

During these musical and choral experiences, we worked with an outstanding array of Canadian artists and composers, such as Maureen Forrester, The Canadian Brass, Nexus Percussion Ensemble, and the popular composer and late Hagood Hardy ("The Homecoming Theme"). These artists embraced our youth choir to perform with them on stage either in Massey Hall or in Roy Thomson Hall. My musical formation was shaped by some of the day's leading performers. Little did I realize how important my acquired musical learning would be in the challenging years to come.

Dr. Elmer Iseler gave TMYC the opportunity to perform with the Toronto Mendelssohn Choir at least once a year. As the "feeder choir," we would be up in the rafters of Massey Hall, performing and singing our hearts out. We always received excellent reviews for our efforts from Toronto's newspaper critics. TMYC was fortunate to celebrate and perform the world premieres of new Canadian compositions by Dr. Derek Holman and by the late and gifted Jewish composer, Srul Irving Glick.

Years after my departure, Cooper and the choir were given the opportunity to tour Vancouver, B.C., as part of Expo 1986 and to travel to Italy. The choir even performed at a Vatican outdoor service for John Paul II during a special mass in 1988.

Robert Cooper is such an outstanding rhythmic machine and conductor. For more than ten years I have sung in his choirs and assisted him with choral administration duties. I have never worked with a conductor who has such a passion for precision in rhythm, diction, interpretation of the choral sound, and the specific colour of tone that he requires from his choirs.

Under the direction of Robert Cooper and TMYC's first choir manager, Kathy Brown, I had the opportunity to explore a variety of career paths in both vocal and choral arts management. I will always be deeply grateful to both Cooper and Brown for their mentorship. They both gave me an exceptional chance to apprentice as chorister, musician, and administrator, soaring to new heights through these valuable real-life read-throughs and dress rehearsals, building my skills.

With Robert Cooper, my friend and mentor for close to forty years!
(ECG Collection)

CHAPTER FOUR
LIVING IN THE SHADOW OF ADD/ADHD

Something was wrong. No matter how hard I tried, when it came to numbers, I couldn't get it. It just didn't make sense. Barely in Grade One at Prince Phillip Public School in Hamilton, Ontario, I was already bumping into the beginnings of having a learning difficulty. I simply couldn't comprehend this new language called math. Fortunately ... but also unfortunately ... math wasn't the focus in the curriculum; reading, or "reading-readiness," was the primary subject. Read—I could do that!

In a classroom with a stronger emphasis on reading, sounding out words phonetically, and learning how to spell, I could manage. Reading, therefore, became my solace and my source of creativity. Without being a good reader, and in some cases "self-educating" myself on varied topics and interests, I don't think that I would have developed a desire to obtain a BA or Master's Certificate in Fundraising. I excelled at reading and loved it. Still do! I enjoyed reading all types of books and stories, and when I was a child, I loved colourful illustrations. My mind could wander and dream of the exciting countries and places I was exploring through books. Who needed numbers when you had words?

Once again, however, numbers came into importance. Moving from Hamilton to neighboring Dundas early in the summer of 1967 required a change of schools. Pleasant Valley Public School had different math expectations of their Grade One students, and, as a result, I was assessed as not having received enough basic Grade One mathematical skills. In hindsight, I should have repeated that grade, but it was decided that I could "catch up on my weak math skills."

Throughout Grades One through Five, I was pushed ahead each year with hopeful comments on my report cards from my teachers that "Ian will improve in his math studies." Instead, things got much worse. It wasn't until the end of Grade Five that the school decided to address my poor math skills.

Mrs. Elizabeth Moore, a Christian and special education teacher, was sent by the Hamilton Board of Education in the early 1970s to observe my progress. She came into my life at a crucial time and was instrumental in helping me find answers to some very difficult and confusing questions concerning my learning issues and solutions to the problems. Mrs. Moore tested my overall academic abilities and coordinated remedial action with mathematics to enhance my skills and maximize my strengths toward an academic future. Using varied testing methods, she determined I had problems with my attention span. She identified me as having a hyperactive attention disorder, now commonly referred to as ADD or ADHD.

Mrs. Moore evaluated my strengths and discussed them with my parents and teachers. The tests revealed that I scored high on intelligence; I was highly artistic by nature and had an aptitude for art, music, and languages. These results indicated that I was capable of advanced academics, even though I didn't do well in math. The tests also indicated that I was socially immature for my age.

From that time on I was labelled as having a learning disability. We had no idea how this unfortunate label would impact my future, self-esteem, and general outlook on life. Being known as hyperactive, and later

ADHD, cast shadows over me throughout my life, causing me a great deal of pain and self-esteem issues. Only my Heavenly Father knows the extent to which this label affected me throughout my childhood, teen years, and adult life.

Eventually I was placed on a medication called Melarill, like Ritalin, and was monitored by our family doctor for two years. Dr. A.C. Helt and I would discuss my ADHD personal symptoms. He would check on the medication that I was taking and if it was making a difference in my home life. Dr. Helt would say to me, "How is life going for you, Ian? Have you had any emotional issues that you want to discuss with me?" He would also tell me to "not drink too much pop, due to the sugar intake." This was excellent advice.

In my mid-teens, I discovered that too much sugar would indeed drastically enhance my hyperactivity and send my ADHD symptoms sky high. Dr. Helt loved our family, and once my mother became a nurse, what Dr. Helt said was law! He was extremely helpful and supportive to our family in seeking out counselling, especially for my parents dealing with an ADD/ADHD child.

At the end of the two years of being on medication, Dr. Helt didn't see improvement in my behaviour and took me off the drug. I was thirteen years old. It was Dr. Helt's suggestion to my parents that they change their approach. He advised that they begin to guide me toward areas of the arts and develop my natural energies and passion to succeed in something that gave me boundless joy! It was also Dr. Helt's suggestion that we have "family counselling." This was excellent advice for my parents raising a disabled child, and subsequent family relationships and communication issues.

After the assessment at Pleasant Valley School, I was assigned to a special education class at Dundas Central Public School where I travelled daily by bus. If it wasn't humiliating enough to be labelled as the kid with a mental disorder, I was yanked out of my former school and friendships and shipped off to a school and a special class where only teens or older students with disorders were sent. It was pure torment.

Their decision initiated the most emotionally traumatic period of my young life. It broke my spirit to be transported every day to this tough, mid-town school. It may not have been an issue for other children, but it was tragic for me. The daily bus commute was approximately forty-five minutes each way. The special education classes in my first year were nothing more than a glorified babysitting service. The teacher was just one year away from retirement and had lost her ambition to assist students with their learning disabilities. I was sent to Central Public School for four complete school terms.

People have asked me what I remember about my childhood being diagnosed with ADHD and being different. I recall being emotionally depressed, like someone was holding me under water and preventing me from breathing or enjoying my life! With these school, home, and general emotional life issues confronting me daily, I felt that I was being blocked from my aspirations of being a musician or performer as my career choice. I was a good student in the courses that I enjoyed, and I even excelled at them. But not so with sports!

I knew I was intelligent; I liked to read, learn, and grow. These ongoing emotional problems stemming from school pressures, bullying, and being a boy with solid artistic tendencies led to depression. I constantly asked myself, "Will this situation ever get better? Will I live in this chaos for the rest of my life?"

Moments of "laughter" helped me to cope at home and at school. Due to the emotional rollercoaster I experienced on school days, I came home very tired and frustrated. My only escape from the taunting, bullying, and occasional fistfights for self defense and solace was between 4:00 and 5:00 p.m. (the *Lucy* programs were on during this time in the afternoon). That's when I entered the world of Lucille Ball through the *I Love Lucy* show on television.

While watching the reruns of this delightful 1950s comedy series, I laughed ... and I laughed some more. I can testify to what the Bible says about humour: "*A happy heart is good medicine and a joyful mind causes healing, but a broken spirit dries up the bones*" (Proverbs 17:22). I relate to that scripture! *I Love Lucy* was like medicine to me!

The painful school experiences and anxiety I endured year after year at Central Public were daily washed away as I laughed hysterically. Lucy's style of comedy soothed my broken spirit and let me forget my pain for just a few hours. I now have the entire *I Love Lucy* series on DVD in my collection. Lucille Ball was, and still is, my favourite comedienne.

In the 1960s, television had a huge influence on our lives. We watched the world changing before our eyes—everything from the tragic assassinations of US President John F. Kennedy, Martin Luther King, and Robert Kennedy to the triumph of the space race. Just like every other young boy in the 1960s, I was fascinated with technology, the space program, and the NASA astronauts landing on the moon.

At my Helmkay grandparents' home we watched every important detail and nuance of Walter Cronkite's well-researched commentary and reporting of these events. We were in awe of the technologically advanced world in which we lived. Neil Armstrong's immortal words rang in my ears: "One small step for man; one giant leap for mankind."

I too took a giant step after being placed in a special education class and then back into a mainstream classroom for Grades Six, Seven, and Eight. It was a giant leap for me to anticipate being in a positive surrounding of the high school of my choice. I looked forward to developing new friendships, took valuable arts courses, and built myself a future career path.

Unfortunately, like a space alien, I just didn't fit in! I wasn't cool, and I was taller and nearly two years older than most of my schoolmates. My interests were in music and the arts, in television and in reading. Sports? Forget it ... wasn't interested! I hated the daily taunting and teasing about being in special education or being called "the giant" because of my size. "How's the weather up there, Ian?" Some people repeated hurtful cliché comments even as I played along, trying to fit in.

Because I was perceived as different, I was also attacked physically. My only choice was to fight back. To help defend myself against the daily bullies, my dad gave me some boxing pointers on how to keep my guard up. At times, it seemed the whole male student body wanted to beat me up.

During the first two years at Central, I grew fearful as the end of each school day approached. I never knew if I would be drawn into a fight or not. Most painful was the daily harassment of being called degrading names. I was repeatedly put down and called "mental" and "stupid," even by some who didn't know me. Developing severe self-hatred and a lack of self-esteem, I regularly had thoughts of suicide.

Wouldn't you know that these same bullies who harassed me in public school would go on to attend Parkside Secondary, just like me? They continued to call me cruel and abusive names day in and day out until I graduated. I recall them now as tormenting classmates with very low IQs. Like sheep, they did what the leader of the group told them to do. Certainly the forces that drove them seemed to be bent on destroying me, my destiny, and God's call on my life. Would the song in my soul be silenced forever?

It wasn't until much later in my thirties and forties when, through counselling, I received healing from the negative emotional and depressive memories. Counselling helped me forgive myself and others who had abused me. I later learned that these memories would require releasing forgiveness to them and later myself.

As a child, I couldn't articulate my emotional distress that arose from attending Central School with its bullying issues. During my therapy sessions, I could openly discuss all these painful memories and have healing and closure. The problem mushroomed, because later in my teen years, I generated discipline issues toward my parents and developed relationship problems with my siblings. I clashed with my sisters, and I resented my brother. He and my dad were very close, and I was envious. I felt rejected and abandoned. I used various tactics to gain self-esteem and acknowledgement.

For example, I abused the power of my status as the oldest male sibling, taking the rage I had suppressed at school and unleashing it on my brother and sisters. I used all this pent-up anger about my life circumstances as hurtful and destructive tactics to impress my siblings with my "superiority." My aggression and tempestuous anger distanced me from my sisters for years. They found it difficult to trust me. Before my parents passed away, I was finally able to share with them the extent of emotional trauma I suffered during those years. My siblings certainly knew about the shadows. It wasn't until I was willing to shed some light on those areas that they could even begin to understand what lurked in those dark places.

CHAPTER FIVE
MY STRATEGIES FOR OVERCOMING THE SHADOWS OF ADHD

As a fifty-year-old survivor of this disorder, I've put together a personal list of strategies to overcome "the ADHD shadow" tendencies in one's family. This list comes from the clarity of hindsight and from shedding some light into those shadows.

1. DEVELOP COMPENSATING SKILLS

For me it was music, and I especially love singing and performing live. Developing these skills helped me cope with many difficult and emotional experiences that affected my self-image. I was (and still am) very comfortable performing, speaking to an audience, or introducing myself to new people. I believe that many people with ADHD are very intelligent and enjoy being out in the public or on the concert stage. Encourage the ADHD student to enjoy whatever it is that they are passionate about:

music, the arts, sports, or education and knowledge. Parents and family members must be encouragers of these varied interests.

2. LISTEN TO MUSIC

Music is my great healer! Listening to music of any kind—gospel, pop, Broadway, classical, choral, or opera—was, and still is, my solace. If the text and rhythm of the music are choral, gospel, or worship, it usually lifts discouragement. When I'm discouraged, or in need of a boost of self-esteem, I also reflect on a wonderful solo and choral career—celebrating "these accomplishments," with goals set and achieved.

Even for the non-musical person, music can be healing therapy. Music therapy builds better focus, self-control, and social skills in kids with ADD or ADHD. Music therapy also reduces hyperactivity. "Music exists in time, with a clear beginning, middle, and end," says Kirsten Hutchison, a music therapist at Music Works Northwest, a non-profit community music school near Seattle. "That structure helps an ADHD child plan, anticipate, and react." [1]

3. READ!

Be a reader or encourage the ADHD child to learn to enjoy reading at whatever level of competency. Being read to as a child, especially picture books, became such an interest for me! These family sessions of "reading before bedtime" opened many creative channels in developing and appreciating the love of language, or learning about other countries, customs, and family relationships. Later, as I became a genuine book person, I developed life skills in research and development. Reading opened the pathway to being self-educated—all by just reading, growing, and learning!

Read suitable and age appropriate content in any form: comic books or closed captions on favourite movies. One technique parents use includes reading one page aloud with the student reading the next. Early on, it may be reading alternate sentences. Reading aloud while recording

[1] Kristen Hutchinson, quoted in Anni Layne Rodgers, "Music Therapy: Sound Medicine for ADHD," *ADDitude: Inside the ADHD Mind*, https://www.additudemag.com/music-therapy-for-adhd-how-rhythm-builds-focus/. (accessed April 2, 2018)

the individual's voice, then following along while listening to that same recording, is effective in correcting reading errors.

4. PRAY! THEN PRAY SOME MORE.

During those stressful times within our family unit, my mother would connect with three other ladies/mothers for prayer, as their sons also had "disability issues." Together they prayed for their sons and for their ongoing issues. I am very grateful for these women who prayed for me for many years, as God did answer their prayers and gave me the ability to advance with strength and stamina throughout my school days.

5. DEVELOP A PERSONAL INTEREST IN A FAMILY PET!

We had a wonderful black female Labrador dog we called Shadow who brought all of us so much love within the family. Shadow seemed to sense when I needed special attention or comfort. She would stay by me when I was having a traumatic day or had a bullying episode coming home from school. We four kids all took care of her needs as part of our weekly allowance and responsibility. Shadow always knew when I needed her to just be there for additional emotional support.

Now my wife Elaine and I have "Faith," a shih-tzu-Havanese brown, tan, and white dog, who helps make our family complete! I had never had a small dog before, and Faith (alias Pumpkin Pie) is very smart at the age of four years old. Faith has her own personality. We both love her very much! I am her principle care-giver, and she and I are very close with lots of cuddle times. Even now as I am typing she is on my lap wanting some loving and attention and, of course … food.

6. DEVELOP AND CREATE A PERSONAL STRATEGY FOR LEARNING AND TEST TAKING.

Persons suffering from ADHD have weaknesses, such as depression, but they also have many strengths. To overcome weaknesses, they develop defense and coping mechanisms that help them handle various aspects of their disorder. For example, my memory is impeded when it comes to academics. I have had to adopt strategies, such as highlighting text and developing retention strategies for tests or exams. I have in the past developed flash cards with important key facts on them to assimilate information.

Because ADHD has also affected my short-term memory, I have carried those same test-taking strategies over into my daily life. At the beginning of each day, I compile a to-do list. More than likely during the day I'll forget what I wanted to accomplish or what was so urgent that needed to be completed. Having a to-do list keeps me on track. There are other areas where I excel. With respect to verbal skills, I can hold my own.

To improve upon my short to long term memory, I remember faces and am trying to improve on learning and retaining names on a daily basis. I love to research when I'm interested in a topic; this skill balances my weak memory for academic pursuits.

7. LEARN ANOTHER LANGUAGE.

I have studied French and German, and I can get by conversationally in French. I have a few dear friends who speak to me in French so that I can still practice using this language. I studied German in high school for later usage in music.

Over the years, I have sung in English, French, German, Spanish, and recently Russian, with professional coaches who have supported me in my vocal or choral diction. With my own youth choir, we've sung in Urdu (this is the national language of Pakistan.), French, and Spanish.

8. ESTABLISH AND MAINTAIN DISCIPLINED ROUTINE AND STRUCTURE.

Was school and studying music a struggle for you? How did you apply these coping mechanisms? I'm asked these questions frequently. For me, having a routine between after school time and homework preparation was certainly key.

When studying music, the only problem that I had (and needed my mom's assistance with) was in breaking down the math in the music. If I had a difficulty with the rhythm, I discovered that once I could read and got the rhythmic pattern in my head, it was then firmly implanted in my memory. That was accomplished by clapping out the rhythm and going over difficult passages repeatedly.

During my teen years, if I'd had a difficult day, Mom would say "Go play the piano; write some new songs or play some hymns and you'll feel much better." This way I programmed my own creative and stress-relieving down time. After an hour or so of composing my own music or playing some hymns, I created my own music therapy session that would calm my nerves. As I managed my emotional triggers with music, I grew in my own confidence as a young pianist and musician. The song in my soul stirred healing as it was about to do for the rest of my life. I had stumbled upon my greatest medicine.

Later, after supper, I would be ready to focus on my homework. If the homework was math, I usually needed my dad's support to get the assignment done. Dad did his best to understand that I couldn't always break down the equation or the math problem, due to my math trauma. But other times he would get mad at me ... until, that is, he learned how to speak my language. By using simple steps in demonstrating and through being generous with encouraging words, he helped me to eventually solve the problem. In courses such as English, Geography, History, French, or the Arts, there was no problem with my learning disability.

9. DEVELOP OTHER INTERESTS.

Life isn't as rich when entirely focused and disciplined around activities that are based solely on the fact that one has ADHD. Find activities that feed the passion to do and do them well! Personal interest and passion open new doors for future growth. Who would guess that having a passion for reading and learning about British history would have such a major impact on me?

On my mother's side of the family, we are "royal watchers and monarchists," with both English and Welsh roots. We can trace our history from 1125, and we are descendants of Edward II. More on this topic in another chapter! I have a deep, personal interest in Royal Family history!

Since childhood, I have loved to read, learn, and study the British Royal Family and our Canadian history—it's my hobby! My personal collection is vast, with the bulk of it on the historical period from Queen Victoria until our present Queen Elizabeth II and her family. I have more than five hundred books, magazines, china, VHS tapes, and DVDs. Time always flies by for me when I look at my Royals' scrapbooks and other items in my collection. I lose myself in this hobby.

My mother and I engaged in ongoing discussions about the current affairs of the British Royal Family. From the time I was nine until she passed away, these encouraging chats and conversations about my interests became my own personal source of pride. I could speak intelligently about my Royal Family interests, which often became an ice breaker for me when chatting with family members on either side of the family. I also developed self-esteem when speaking knowledgably about my collection.

In 2010, the now classic film *The King's Speech* gained world acclaim. It starred Colin Firth as King George VI, and Helena Bonham-Carter as Queen Elizabeth, the Queen Consort. Geoffrey Rush filled the role of Lionel Logue, the amazing speech therapist who aided the King to overcome his own speech disability. The King was required by his position to broadcast speeches of information and support to the world in the days leading up to the Second World War.

This film had a deep impact on me as I reflected on my own frustrations as a child into adulthood. I reflected on my struggles, working for many years with tutors or specialists that helped me develop my own voice in overcoming my disability issues. Like the King's family as the basis of his support, I had my parents, family members, and others who stood by me throughout the decades.

At the end of the film, there is a dual scene of Logue coaching George VI word by word and empowering and supporting him to make this historic speech on September 3, 1939. It is very emotional for me to watch this scene. Just like the King, I know the stamina and effort it takes to overcome a speech disability in a public setting.

I reflected on my own memories and times of adversity throughout my whole life— overcoming the loss of jobs, writing and editing difficult academic papers, or studying for exams with hopes of achieving my best, but failing. There were many circumstances where I didn't fit in. I realized how similar my experiences were to George VI's. I had extraordinary emotional support of family members, but I had the added advantage of those loved ones praying for me to overcome the daunting roadblocks of self-esteem and be firmly established on the road to personal achievement.

From the negative and fearful emotions I experienced as a child in public school, I too developed a slight stutter when speaking in public. As I advanced in my voice lessons, my speaking voice improved naturally as I learned to breathe properly from my diaphragm. Thus, my nervousness of public speaking disappeared.

In 2010, I had the opportunity to speak at Parkside High School to the graduating class and to our international alumni for their fiftieth anniversary reunion celebration. It was a breakthrough for me to speak publicly about my life and career, with good breathing techniques along with a little humour thrown in. Lionel Logue was correct in establishing proper breathing techniques to overcome speech difficulties and fears.

An earlier time when my special interest in the British monarchy and history was of benefit was during my second year in special education. That was when Lieutenant Colonel Roy Schmidt, retired from the Canadian Armed Forces, became my new teacher. Mr. Schmidt took command of the classroom. He had a zero-tolerance approach to nonsense, and very soon we became a small Schmidt army. Many students in Schmidt's class were destined to continue to trade school. Except for me. I dreamed of attending high school and then university.

From this time in Mr. Schmidt's class, we would begin to see God's provisions and answers to my parents' prayers. We began to have renewed hope for the development of my education and passion and future career in the arts! I now view my time with Mr. Schmidt as divinely appointed.

Mr. Schmidt noticed I had strong grounding in geography, history, literature, and the arts, and that I knew and could retain vast amounts of historical data. Once in conversation, I proved to Schmidt the details of what I knew about the British Royal Family and the Canadian and Commonwealth government structures. Impressed by my retention of data, he jump-started the process of getting me out of the special education classroom and back into the rotary system. Schmidt then created a special curriculum for me, which allowed me to learn additional subjects at a Grade Six level. He arranged for my math class to be a tutored course in the rotary program. In 1973, I was assessed as being able to re-join the Grade Six curriculum and continue toward high school. My knowledge of the British Royal Family saved me from being placed in a vocational school! It's important to understand that ADHD does not necessarily indicate low intelligence; in fact, some studies suggest that ADHD often correlates to a higher level of creativity.[2]

During his entire teaching career, Mr. Schmidt had seen only two special needs students re-enter the regular curriculum. I was the second. He was thrilled with my progress. Schmidt came personally to visit our family to tell us the excellent news that I could continue my schooling toward high school. God's grace was on us. We rejoiced!

10. KEEP A JOURNAL.

Make a concerted effort to keep a journal of a younger child's ADHD emotional journey. There are very few notes or written comments on my school report cards as to my ADHD emotional journey. Notes or brief entries in a journal, describing the emotional climate of the child, the household, sibling issues, or medication taken or not taken, would have been very helpful in building a stronger relationship with our family doctor or specialist.

Encourage the very young child to journal with pictures and drawings of emotions and feelings. Let the child know that expressing this way is healthy and helpful. Keep those journals in a safe place and in confidence.

11. DILIGENTLY CHECK OPTIONS OTHER THAN, OR TO COMPLEMENT, PRESCRIBED MEDICATION.

I'm not a doctor and do not pretend to know all the ins and outs of children being exposed to high doses of chemicals for their ADHD issues, yet I have some deep concerns for ADHD family members who have been overly medicated with Ritalin, as there are recent studies coming

---

[2] Scott Barry Kaufman, "The Creative Gifts of ADHD," *Scientific American,* https://blogs.scientificamerican.com/beautiful-minds/the-creative-gifts-of-adhd/. (accessed April 2, 2018).

out about adults with ADHD. I am greatly concerned about the future emotional well-being for young students who have been highly exposed to Ritalin and other drugs designed to suppress their ADHD symptoms. My new personal motto in this discussion is "music vs. medicine." I personally know that this technique has worked for me!

Check out all the different options (including diet) and research these prescribed drugs and their side-effects as well as explore different therapies with your family doctor or certified specialists.

12. REALIZE THAT ADHD IS A FAMILY PROBLEM AND REQUIRES FAMILY INVOLVEMENT FOR SOLUTIONS.

My memories of the family therapy sessions are somewhat sketchy. I do remember that the six of us had to express our opinions about intimate family matters. Our family therapy specialists also wanted to know how our faith influenced our family life and how we related with each other.

To observe my interaction with my siblings, they asked us to draw and play with toys they had assembled in an observation room. My father told me that I drew black crayoned pictures of death and destruction consistent with the emotional state of a very depressed young boy.

The doctors sat behind a one-way mirror and recorded our conversations. They asked many probing questions, taking notes on our interactions to understand how our family functioned. These sessions helped me express my feelings and cope with negative thoughts and emotions. As a result, our communication improved. We learned to listen to each other as a family; we learned to interact in love and respect each other and to express ourselves openly and freely, whether we agreed or disagreed.

13. SPEND SOME QUALITY TIME WITH DAD

Spending that one-on-one time with Dad was very important. Dad encouraged me to have a guy-thing, an "outdoor fort." I discussed the plans with my dad to build my fort at the ravine of our property, going for that "in the wild" setting. Our family business was sheet metal and we obtained a ready supply of wooden shipping crates stacked outside our shop. These crates inspired me to create my own design as a fort.

I was not at all interested in the traditional tree fort—that would have been too common. I wanted something unique, like a fort in a triangular "A-frame" shape, such as something you might see in a *Better Forts and Gardens* magazine.

Despite all the emotional chaos inside me, with a saw, hammer, and many nails, we built this triangular fort together when I was eleven years old. Dad gave me his blessing and his guidance in building this structure, regardless of how I wanted it to be! His only concern was that the fort withstand the potentially severe winter weather of Southern Ontario.

We constructed the A-frame for the fort with a cool looking window in the middle of two supporting walls. I decorated it with discarded furniture I had picked up from some garage sales. I then designed a flag and pole (like the Queen's when she's in residence) that I could hoist when I was in residence. Spending afternoons alone, or with my brother sleeping overnight, in my fort helped connect me to the normal side of life as an adventurous child. During those times, I felt like I was a normal kid. The darkness that constantly overshadowed my school days dissipated. The fort survived for at least ten years, giving my brother and me a great deal of pleasure before it became an eyesore and had to be demolished.

In recalling this time in my life, I realize that I took on a lot of guilt and shame, which wouldn't be resolved until my adult therapy sessions. I felt bad that my ADHD problems caused additional pressure on my parents. I also believed that I had brought a pox on the family name by having this disorder. I just did not like myself!

Not all my times with Dad were so positive. For twenty-five years, my dad had been involved in scouting and was the head scout master in our local Hamilton scout troop. From being a cub scout, I loved the experience of being with boys my own age, playing some sports, and gaining many badges—except, of course, for tying knots. That task of tying knots remains something that my dexterity or memory doesn't compute. I was particularly uncoordinated, or perhaps a memory issue caused a momentary blank-out. I have since discovered that a lack of coordination for a child can be a symptom of ADHD.

Having a dad as head scout leader was difficult enough ... but being involved with his troop in my teens was even harder. "Scouting" portrayed an image much like that of a testosterone-driven army dude and appealed to the macho side of teen boys with its promises of adventure, thrills, challenges, and independence. The idea of jumping off a cliff suspended by a pulley of rope, or perhaps dangling over a rapidly moving stream, like on a poster with a caption stating, "Come Join the Army," might as well have said, "Come Join Scouting." For me, that was a problem.

Experiencing the traditional masculine and adventurous side of life was not for me, even though my dad was a scout leader. But I had no choice. In the dead of a Canadian winter, we packed our camping gear and headed out on a survival weekend. The plan was for us to endure a two-day event in a poorly-insulated, unheated summer cottage, and live to tell about it. There were almost twenty of us in an open room as we spread our sleeping bags next to a roaring fire that needed to be stoked throughout the night. Some of the guys snored and kept me awake most of the night as the fire dwindled. Of course, nobody woke to tend it, so when we got up the next morning, the fire was out.

As I recall, one of the senior scouts was recruited to tend to the fire. Dad supervised the activity as we all stood around jumping up and down, trying to get warm. I was freezing and tired. At that time, I was growing profusely and needed a balanced rest and an exercise routine. If my sleep was interrupted and I didn't get eight hours or more, I'd feel nauseous and grumpy.

On this cold Saturday morning, after breakfast, we trekked out into the snow, where the young scouts were to be initiated. This initiation involved walking across a stream on a snow-covered broken tree limb of about six to eight feet in diameter. Ice cold, freezing water coursing over rocks and under ice patches added to the feel of danger. Standing on the log, I froze in fear.

With only a rope tied around my waist and depending only on the leaders for support and rescue, I shivered while awaiting my turn on the tree branch. I fought back against frightening mental images. I could easily imagine falling off the log, plunging into the icy water ready to sweep me further downstream. I could imagine myself frantically clinging to the rope for dear life while everyone else stood on the shore, laughing. I shook my head, trying to be free of the terrifying images. *I'll embarrass my dad*, I panicked. *I can't do it! Will he dive in to save me if I fall off the log?* My dad, facing me on the opposite side of the stream, recognized terror on my face and yelled encouraging words. "Ian, you can do it! Come on! You can do it!"

Fear nearly took my breath away. I looked at my dad for support and was determined that I was going to get through this frightening experience. I walked slowly on the icy log then, crouching carefully, I crawled on all fours toward my dad's voice. I teetered from side to side until I got to the end of the log. Overcome with adrenalin and relief at the same time, I kissed the snowy earth, glad to have survived this ordeal! I was so glad to be back on solid ground, but my stomach was in knots.

Feelings of guilt and shame rushing like Niagara Falls overwhelmed any triumph I might feel. Paralyzed by fear that I might embarrass my dad, I spent most the remainder of this adventure in sheer panic of what might come next. As the weekend progressed, I couldn't eat and felt increasingly nauseous. I knew my father couldn't handle anyone throwing up. If one of us kids got sick, he'd feel sick and insist Mom take over and clean up the sick child. As it turned out, I ended up with a memorable case of diarrhea and learned all about survival in a frozen outhouse. It may seem comical now, but at the time it was sheer terror.

Toward the end of this wild and less-than-wonderful weekend, I developed a slight fever. During an evening's outing in this winter paradise, I was still nauseous, and the jostling of the car didn't help. Suddenly, a horrible sensation arose deep inside. I barely got the window down before I wretched all over the side of the car—someone else's car, of course … not ours. Poor Dad! He had to clean it up with some snow. He was almost sick himself.

That did it. Enough of this "male bonding" adventure. I quit scouting shortly after. Once again, the teasing began, and I was now known as "barf boy." From then on, I was determined to be known as a "city boy" with all the comforts of civilization right at hand. My dad and I would often reminisce about that winter camping experience we shared as father and son. It was one of our few common memories that we shared together.

In Grade Seven at Central Public School, I was involved in a "semi"-rock band and needed a tambourine. Dad and I priced what one might cost, and it seemed very expensive. He suggested we make our own out of sheet metal and involved me in the process. Dad created the framework, and then we cut metal pieces, joining them together so that it shimmered and shone like any normal percussion instrument. I used that tambourine for many years. This experience and the instrument meant a lot to me. I felt Dad's love for me, and it gave me a taste of his skill as a craftsman. Over the years, I have experienced the passionate love of our "Father God." Just like my natural father, Bill, my Heavenly Daddy has been there for me, surrounding me with His goodness, His presence, His love, His joy, and His power in my life.

Just as my dad created that perfect, customized instrument of joy, God pulled all the necessary components together in my life. My emotional well-being has been healed now, and for the remaining years of my life, I want nothing more than to be a worshipper, leading others in praises of song and continuous service to Him.

14. ADHD IS NOT AN EXCUSE FROM LEARNING RESPONSIBILITY AND ETHICS!

In addition to Dad being a great craftsman and hard worker, he instilled an excellent work ethic in all his children. He believed that no matter what we would eventually end up doing with our lives, we should be skilled in sales and customer service.

During our teen years, we three began a very successful paper route as a part-time business. Each sibling took it over from the older one. Andrew, the youngest, followed our steps with over twenty-five years of service with this paper route. We had at least one hundred customers, and my dad was insistent that we give good customer service. Dad had a successful paper route as a teenager, where he learned the beginnings of being self-employed and independent. At the beginning of this venture, Dad demonstrated a common-sense approach for us three in maintaining our customer base.

Regardless of the weather, we had to deliver our newspapers, and we weren't allowed to miss a customer should a paper suddenly disappear or be missed. On occasion, if the weather was especially bad, our parents drove us around our route.

Just before one Christmas, our customers were very generous and gave me as much as $200 in tips for excellent service throughout the year. For us this was not only great money, but the job taught us how to handle finances, how to run a business, and how to develop good customer relations. Each of us developed friendships with our customers that have continued even until today.

These early sales training experiences and business discussions with Dad laid a foundation between us. My sales, public relations, and arts marketing career all began with this initial venture. Both my parents were great mentors who imparted to me an entrepreneurial spirit.

15. DEVELOP AND VALUE CLOSE FRIENDSHIPS.

Developing close friendships with other boys was hard for me once I was in Grades Seven and Eight. Much taller and two years older than most, I chummed around with a few male friends. Despite my musical abilities, I was also a gangling scarecrow at that time. Uncoordinated and un-athletic, I did enjoy running. One friend, Bill Bynum, became my close public school friend and has remained my best buddy since 1972. Bill was a pianist, musician, and academic. When he had a certain fun-filled gleam in his eye, you knew that he was up to something! Bill was good at track and field, and I was envious of his abilities.

Together we enjoyed composing songs, much like Elton John and Bernie Taupin, whom we both liked and listened to endlessly. We tried to emulate their style. We composed around ten songs together, some of them great, and others bad by today's standards. We hung out at each other's houses at opposite ends of the Dundas ravine and walked it many times.

We had a sense of humour only the two of us could appreciate. One of my best memories is of laughing together as we watched Alfred Hitchcock's *The Birds*. At the most frightening scenes when the music intensified, Bill made jokes about the hapless victims on the screen, and I laughed hysterically. Sick humour, but it was great!

Bill was always welcome at our house. We joked that Bill would have a knack of knowing when to arrive; he would arrive precisely at dessert time when a delicious piece of pie or cake was being served. Together we were involved in youth or musical activities at the nearby Baptist churches, especially at Ancaster Baptist, where youth ages fifteen to mid-twenties enjoyed games, sports, and musical activities as well as Bible studies. Bill's friendship meant a lot to me during my dark and depressive days at Central Public School. He made me laugh and feel like "one of the boys." I don't know what might have become of me without his friendship. Today "Mr. Bill" is faithfully serving the Lord as a pastor of a local Ontario congregation.

16. DEVELOP A PERSONAL RELATIONSHIP WITH JESUS CHRIST.

Having a personal and daily relationship with God changes everything! The same year Bill and I became close friends, I also made friends with someone else—Jesus Christ. Being raised in a Christian household didn't give me a ticket to Heaven and eternal salvation. I had to experience a personal commitment to God myself.

Grant Helmkay and I had been together as cousin campers at Camp Oneida, a summer Baptist camp on Lake Erie, for two consecutive years, but now there was a problem. Uncle Norman's family was moving from Canada to the States, and Grant was to leave camp about four days early. It would be a very long time until our two families would be reunited. With thoughts that my cousin, Grant, was going to leave me all by myself, I experienced deep loneliness and fear. When Grant left camp early, the dreaded feelings of loneliness and fear gripped me. My ADHD anxieties again tainted what was intended to be a joyful experience. Camp officials knew of my passion for "music making," so they kept me busy singing, playing the piano, and encouraging me to help lead in campfire activities.

Christine (known as Chris) Field, a dear family friend, was one of the founders of Camp Oneida. She was one of the mothers that met to pray for their sons dealing with various disability issues. I considered Chris a trusted friend. By chance, or by design, she was visiting the camp and had stayed for dinner and the evening's devotions. When the invitation was given for anyone to come forward who wanted to turn their life over to Jesus as their Saviour, I responded. After all, I reasoned, Grant had left me and I needed a friend. Neither did I want these feelings of fear and loneliness to remain with me for the rest of camp, let alone for my life.

I stepped forward and Chris was there to walk me through the steps of becoming a new believer. Something happened to me that night. I was twelve years old and my life was transformed. After this encounter with God and before the end of camp, I remember the peace and tranquilly I felt. I wasn't afraid anymore, and I began to mingle with others. Once I surrendered my life to the Lord, the realization that I could leave behind these negative mental thoughts and emotions attaching themselves to me was the beginning of freedom. As I grew older and wiser in my Christian walk, I had the power to make the negative spirits leave my presence.

As I have said, I believe that my DNA was created to serve, worship, and be passionate about Jesus, the Word of God, and His people. I believe these events were in God's unfolding plan for me and my future career!

CHAPTER SIX
GROWING PAINS, GRADUATION, AND HIGH SCHOOL

In the fall of 1973, I began sixth grade studies in a regular rotary classroom then graduated from eighth grade in 1976. I was finally on my way to high school!

I learned a great deal about Canadian history from my public-school teacher, Mr. Norman Madill. Although he encouraged my passion for the arts, he suggested that I consider history as a future university major. Despite my learning disability, I did very well in the subject—so well, in fact, that at my eighth-grade commencement, I was awarded a second prize for my academic standing in history. In 2005, I watched with pride as my daughter, Christina, received an award at her Grade Eight commencement. I was reminded of my own achievement.

Finishing public school and heading toward high school and then university, I knew that I wanted to major in music. While other boys chose sports as their extracurricular activities, I preferred being in the school dramatic society. In 1973, as part of the music department, I was offered the opportunity to perform and sing the lead role as Captain Corcoran in the student version of Gilbert and Sullivan's *H.M.S. Pinafore*, and in 1976 I was cast as Oscar Lister in *Get Up and Go*, a fun musical about how the old-world values of a former English boys' school modernizing to become co-educational. These were my first experiences playing "older men" characters. In later years, I continued to enjoy those same roles in other theatrical productions.

At Central Public School, Mr. Floyd McAsh, our music teacher, saw vocal talent in me and encouraged me to sing at assemblies and other school events. He became my vocal coach. That's when singing and performing really became my passion.

In my graduation year of 1976, I was in a typical awkward stage, as I was growing by leaps and bounds and was well over six feet tall! I tried my best to fit in and to be like all the other guys who were interested in sports. Due to my age and height, I was often asked, "Do you play basketball?" When I said no, assuming they thought less of me because I didn't play sports, I felt judged. I was asked if I played basketball so many times that I finally gave it a shot. Unfortunately, at sixteen, it was probably too small an effort and too late in my youthful experience to improve upon this athletic skill.

Had I applied myself earlier in public school, I might have played on some teams, but my effort didn't last. One day while I was playing basketball in gym class, I twisted an ankle. The pain was horrendous, but Mom thought that I was faking and didn't take me to the doctor. I walked on that broken foot for six weeks until Mom finally took me to the hospital and discovered that indeed the foot was broken. It had developed into a "green stitch fracture" on the side of my left foot. I needed a plaster cast, and Mom felt terrible! You know, I milked that incident for many years to come. I heaped the guilt on Mom for not believing me as to the truth of the injury; she was, after all, a nurse!

The 1970s and early 1980s were great fun-filled years for our family. We travelled all over Canada and some parts of the States in our tent-trailer. We would be camping and sometimes run into a convoy of my parents' church friends so that we all could be together at the same campsite. What memories these events held! Our family became a tight-knit unit, travelling together as we three kids read many books in the car. During our trek through the prairies and out to the Rocky Mountains and back, I read eight books. We would also sing camp songs or family favourites in the car.

As we all grew older, sometimes we'd sing in harmony. Despite all the painful experiences in public school, my home remained a secure place to grow up. All too soon Anne and I reached the age when we needed to have summer jobs and were no longer a part of the annual family vacations.

***

In June 2007, I had the opportunity to go back to Central Public School to be involved in their 150th anniversary and reunion weekend. I wanted to see from an adult perspective whether the "monsters in the closet" that had sneered at me and taunted me in my younger years with fear were still there.

As I walked around the old and new parts of the school, fleeting memories of the old special ed classroom returned—flashbacks of some painful and negative moments. In the schoolyard, I sensed again a momentary faint impression of voices goading me, a passing sensation of pain from cutting words and fists pounding. I was accompanied by my wife, Elaine, and we walked around as I introduced her to my old school chums and teachers. Some of the old classrooms, including the old special education room where I spent many unhappy hours, were gone. Two beautiful, antique wooden staircases and banisters had been removed due to current fire regulations. A great disappointment!

I desperately wanted to walk into that old special ed classroom and speak forcibly to the walls that, through God's grace, I'd made it! Instead, I laid my hands on the walls and spoke out loud (at the spot that would have connected the old part to the new part of the school.) Interestingly enough, the old fears and negative memories all departed!

CHAPTER SEVEN
FOLLOWING IN THE ARTISTIC FOOTSTEPS OF THE RASHLEIGH FAMILY

I introduced you to Grandma Violet (Rashleigh) Helmkay Garbutt. She taught me so many wonderful things about our Rashleigh family tree and about music, gardening, and life. What I didn't know then was how important a solid family life and interaction would have for me. I was loved and I belonged. Now that my mother has passed, staying in contact with my Uncle Norman (Helmkay) and his family plus my Rashleigh cousins is very important to me!

The Rashleighs are one of Cornwall's great historic families. They can trace their family tree back to 1125. The Rashleighs of Fowey and Menabilly were powerful merchants in the time of Henry VIII and Elizabeth I. Philip Rashleigh of Cury (died 1551) came from Barnstaple in Devon. He became wealthy through trade and was the father of Robert and John. (If you are interested in learning more about this English family history, Google "the Rashleigh's of Menabilly.")

Great-Uncle Norman, Aunt Olive, Uncle Leonard, and Violet (Walker Family Photo

My Rashleigh family connections all lived their faith and had an unmistakable zest for life. They were always welcoming, looking you straight in the eye and speaking directly to you. This warm hospitality really applies to my grandmother's family. Grandma Violet and I performed many times together, beginning when I was a boy soprano to a seasoned baritone soloist. Grandma was the one who initially read Bible stories to us and taught us all how to pray.

Violet was a modern-day intercessor. Violet just bonded with her grandchildren and passed on her Christian legacy to all of us. She taught me how one conducts oneself as an artist in worship. Grandma created and shared many wonderful moments of laughter and fun by listening with compassion. The sad thing was that in Violet's later years, she was deaf in both ears, which was a shared family flaw.

Violet Annie (Rashleigh) Helmkay was born in May of 1903. Along with the Rashleigh family, she emigrated from Newquay, Cornwall (England) to Canada in 1906. As a family of faith, they were Anglican; however, once they came and settled in Toronto, they found a nearby

Baptist church, and my great-grandparents wanted to raise their family in this new denominational setting. Violet told me that my great-great grandfather (George Charles Rashleigh, 1849–1911) was a cantor in the Church of England, Cornwall—the artistic family genes for music and the vocal arts! William John Rashleigh, known as Wills (my great grandfather), was a cabinet maker in England. When he immigrated to Toronto in 1906, he worked for the Toronto Transit Commission (TTC) as a trolley driver.

Violet, George, Norman, Olive, and Leonard were raised with very strict rules within the house. They were not allowed to dance, go to the movies, or play cards. One time in my early teens, we coaxed Grandma to get up and dance with us. Violet was in her early seventies. She danced in the style that resembled the Charleston. It was a fun, memorable time.

Violet and Charlie Helmkay loved young people. I don't remember Grandpa loving to play games as much as Grandma did. We would have great family times. Violet loved to play PIT, UNO, Scrabble, Crazy Eights, and Monopoly. With her knowledge of reading and her great vocabulary, she was a formidable Scrabble opponent. When we would visit my grandparents, we would have family devotions after breakfast. Grandma would read aloud the daily Bible reading. We would join Grandma and Grandpa in their family prayers.

Grandma's wonderful talents in the kitchen blessed all of us. In the 1920s, Violet was a book binder, and in the 1940s she worked as a part-time baker. She perfected her artistry in baking scrumptious breads, muffins, cookies, and other English treats that would make your mouth salivate. Violet's culinary skills were evident right up until her eighty-ninth birthday.

Both Violet and Olive were required to house clean and assist with the cooking duties for the family. My great-grandmother, Florence Mabel Dymond Rashleigh, was a mid-wife in west Toronto. When she would be called out to aid young mothers, Florence left Violet in charge of all the household duties. I can relate. When Mom went back to school for nursing studies in the mid-1970s, she taught all of us to cook and house clean.

LEARNING MUSICAL SKILLS FROM BOTH MY MOTHER AND GRANDMA

Just before I returned for another year at Central Public School, Grandma Violet encouraged me to sing. She gave me practical techniques in interpreting the text and vocal dynamics. My mother would coach me on the rhythm, and Grandma would then refine my performance. Grandma was the organist of St. John's Road Baptist Church, Toronto, for twenty-five years.

Grandma strongly encouraged me to sing and nurture my natural talent. Both my mom and Grandma were always on the lookout for the latest music to challenge me. Grandma would say to Mom, "Oh, Ian could sing this piece beautifully." She witnessed all the emotional turmoil that I was dealing with in public school and into high school. Grandma encouraged my parents to give me weekly voice lessons, which created positive results. This was perhaps the earliest indicator that music had a restorative impact on me and my ADHD.

Before we would sing or worship together in a church service, Grandma would pray and ask God to bless the service and the worship time. Grandma said to me, "Ian, remember to whom you are singing. It is not for yourself that you have been asked to minister today. I am training you to be sensitive in the ways of the Lord." Her words would speak such truth and assurance. I don't remember ever getting nervous when Grandma and I ministered together. Grandma taught me how to be humble and to understand that I was His instrument.

During my teen years, I enjoyed spending some wonderful weekends with my grandparents. In conclusion, I was blessed knowing that there were many people praying for me (my parents, grandparents, and my mother's prayer group). Such support gave me inner peace.

MY BONDING YEARS WITH GRANDPA "CHARLIE" HELMKAY

My grandpa's favourite song was "He Touched Me" by Bill and Gloria Gaither. The presence of God would fall in the room every time I would sing this anointed song. In 1970, Grandpa Charlie was diagnosed with colon cancer.

As he was recuperating at their home from surgery, Grandpa, Grandma, and I would sing the chorus together. Knowing his time with us and the family was short, Grandpa would start to cry. Our family linked arms with him, asking God to heal him. Charlie went home to be with the Lord in October 1972. We didn't understand why Grandpa wasn't healed, but the peace we had surpassed our understanding.

Charlie knew that God had given me a voice to sing. When Grandpa was so sick and dying of cancer, I would stay over at their home. I remember Grandpa telling me how proud he was of me. He felt I was destined for wonderful things. I am so grateful for Grandpa and for the love that he poured out. He blessed my identity. His words of encouragement brought healing to my wounded spirit.

When I graduated from McMaster University on June 8, 2009, at Hamilton Place, I wore one of my Grandpa's favourite burgundy ties. I wanted to consciously bless his memory. I know Charlie would have been very proud of me.

After his passing in 1973, I remembered all the wonderful chats that he and I had shared. Grandpa's death left a deep hole in my young life. My times spent with both my grandparents motivated me to compose the music, and my friend, Bill Bynum, wrote the lyrics to "Vanishing Horizon."

"Vanishing Horizon"

Written in loving memory of my amazing grandfather,
Charles M. Helmkay
Lyrics by William A. Bynum & Music by W. Ian Walker

The time I knew you well,
Was so many years ago,
But even then, I didn't know you.
I couldn't show my love,
Because my love for you was not.
It was always there,
And yet it was not.

CHORUS

You're like a vanishing horizon,
Reappearing in my mind;
Your memory never leaves me.
You're like a vanishing horizon,
And the sounds of you are there;
And only if we had more time,
The things that we could have shared.
You were my closest friend;
My saddened heart will mend.
I wish we had shown our love for one another,
And through the coming years,
My eyes will fill with tears,
Because your memory never leaves me.

CHORUS

LEARNING MORE ABOUT THE RASHLEIGH FAMILY TREE

Grandma Violet used to tell me all the time, "You are so like my family with your Cornish good looks, dark hair, and olive skin." In my mid-teens, I was over six feet tall. Grandma was taught by her parents how to be a good hostess. Grandma had beautiful china, silverware, and a silver tea service. She set a proper table, prepared a good English tea, and passed on this tradition of gracious hospitality.

One of the tender stories that I loved to hear was about when Grandma and Aunt Olive went back to Newquay, Cornwall in the mid-1980s. Violet had not been back to England for over sixty years. Violet and Olive always enjoyed each other's company, so they decided to return to the family store/homestead. Aunt Olive and Uncle Charlie knew where the family store was located. Recognizing the exact place by the molding on the building, Olive and Violet stood in the archway of this family home and had their picture taken. It brought back many memories for both sisters.

As the eldest in the family, Violet lived into her ninety-first year, and on December 26, 1993, she passed away into the loving arms of her Saviour. Grandma was everything to me—mentor, musician, and intercessor. She gave the most wonderful hugs! Her passing required a real adjustment for me.

Violet's siblings were artistic. Two of my great uncles (George and Leonard) were pianists and organists. Uncle Norman appreciated the artistry of a good pianist, though he was not one himself. George and Leonard initially followed in the tradition of playing by ear, as my great-grandfather, Wills Rashleigh, had done.

Violet used to play a piece of music called "Scottish Pastiche" for her father. He loved it. Violet memorized it all, except the middle part. Grandma would play the piece over and over, trying to remember how it went. As I grew to love the piece myself, I composed a new section that I can still play today.

At our family gatherings, Grandma or Uncle Len would be at the organ or piano, and they would start to sing either hymns of the church or popular songs. It was such a grand time to be a spectator! Grandma or Uncle Len would be playing, and I would assist them by turning the pages. As I got older and learned these tunes and the lyrics, I could join in and sing harmony.

Great-Uncle George was the eldest son, and I have a few memories of being around him and my Aunt Louise. Uncle George adored my mother, Doreen, and she adored him equally. He would say, "The sun rose and set on her." George owned and operated his own business renting summer cottages on Lake Muskoka near Gravenhurst, ON. When I was between eleven and twelve years old, we would go and visit Uncle George and his family and stay at one of his cottages. The water was so blue. The swimming area was first rate! I remember Uncle George's smile and those "Rashleigh eyes" that twinkled and shone so brightly.

George, Norman, and Leonard Rashleigh all loved cars. They all were quite handy with fixing any household or automotive problems. In their teenage years, George could be aggressive toward his sister, Violet. Just like any sibling rivalry, they had their moments, but they were also very close right up to George's death in 1977. Around this time, George told Violet he had given his heart to the Lord. Violet was so happy to hear this news, as she had prayed and asked God to save him for over twenty years. All of Violet's siblings had made a personal commitment to Christ. It was very important to Violet that the family circle would be all together in Heaven.

Uncle George loved to play golf, and out on the green one day he had a sudden massive heart attack and died. He was the first of the Rashleigh sons to pass away so early in his retirement years.

Great-Uncle Norman was involved with musical productions at Calvary Baptist Church in the east end of Toronto. These productions were a part of the men's Bible class, which had sixty members. Norman was a master electrician and supervisor of electrical maintenance at the headquarters of the Bank of Commerce in downtown Toronto. He loved to watch Hollywood-style musicals. At Expo 1967, Norman met his musical and entertainment idol, Bing Crosby, and his wife. The Crosbys were in Montreal as tourists, and Norman recognized him. It was a wonderful opportunity for Norman to connect with the legendary crooner. Uncle Norman shared with his family that meeting Crosby was a special moment in his life. Norman was also given the honour of having his nephew (my uncle) and his son named after him, giving us three "Normans" in the family.

I had no idea at that tender age that what I was learning at the feet of Grandma Violet and in interacting with the Rashleigh family would one day become one of the most powerful tools I could use to pull myself out of the grips of ADHD. I was loved and truly appreciated for who I am!

SPENDING TIME WITH AUNT OLIVE AND UNCLE CHARLIE IN MEAFORD, ON

Great-Aunt Olive was an accomplished soloist, pianist, and organist as well as a full-time registered nurse. When Olive married Charlie Knight and started her family in Meaford, she continued her nursing career. She was a very accomplished painter for many years within the Owen Sound/ Grey Bruce Region of Ontario. Two of her paintings were hung for a season in the Tom Thomson Gallery in Collingwood, Ontario.

In the summer of 1977, I stayed with Aunt Olive and Uncle Charlie in their home while I was working as a summer Youth Corps worker. I had only met my Aunt Olive a few times at our family reunions and celebrations; however, when we connected during those early weeks in Meaford, her personality was so much like Violet's, we bonded very quickly. I so enjoyed being around the piano and singing hymns with Olive and learning from her about our Rashleigh family history.

Olive asked me if I would like to go with her into the countryside to sketch. On a warm July summer day, we sketched together. Olive taught and encouraged me with new drawing techniques. I asked Olive how she would get these ideas and colours from her outline onto a new painting. That evening, Olive showed me how to transfer these ideas onto a canvas.

We also talked about the Group of Seven artists, especially Emily Carr. All were favourites of Olive's. From those talks about different Canadian artists, I developed a deep respect and appreciation for the works of Emily Carr. Today I have many books and catalogues in my collection about Carr's art. Who would guess that in the early 1980s, two of the grandchildren of Olive and Charlie Knight, Jordan and Jonathan Knight, would become international super stars with their group, New Kids on the Block (NKOTB)?

Allison, Sharon, David Christopher, Jonathan, and Jordan are the grandchildren. The Knight grandchildren are my second cousins once removed. Allan, their dad, is my second cousin. It's hard to fathom that these two brothers and their group, NKOTB, are as famous as the Beatles!

Aunt Olive was fortunate to attend one of the NKOTB Toronto concerts in the 1980s. Their music was very loud, but it didn't affect Olive, who was mostly deaf. I was told she enjoyed the "spectacular event" by just watching the crowds of young people interact with her grandchildren. I had the opportunity to meet Jordan and Jonathan at a family wedding in the 1990s. We recently had an awesome family reunion backstage in Toronto in June of 2015.

Olive Knight with her grandchildren: Jordan, Allison, Jonathan, and Sharon at a family wedding in the 1990s (Walker Family Photo Collection)

Having some great "family time" with my Knight and Kunica cousins backstage during NKOTB Toronto concert 2015 (ECG Photo Collection)

Uncle Leonard was the last surviving member of the five Rashleigh siblings. He died in January 2007 in his ninety-third year. Uncle Len was a quiet man. He was a well-loved member of the family. Leonard initially was interested in scientific research and in chemical engineering. In his mid-forties to fifties, he began to expand on his carpentry and mechanical skills. Len could fix or build just about anything! My Aunt Irene was a character, and she always had the best stories to make you laugh. Len and Irene were together for fifty plus years until she passed away in 2002.

Being a man of faith, Uncle Len was very supportive of his home church of Oakwood Baptist Church in East Toronto. He attended the Sunday school classes and transported the elderly and the shut-ins to church. Always on the organ/piano at our family events, Len took organ and theory lessons in his early years of retirement in the 1990s.

Len encouraged his sister, Violet, to use all the stops on the organ. Due to his talent and passion, he could make Grandma's home organ "talk." Uncle Len worked on his RCM theory requirements. In his eighties he took his Grades One to Three History and Harmony studies. Len achieved an 80 per cent average. After falling and breaking his hip when he was eighty-eight, his family decided that he needed to be in a Brampton nursing home. Living nearby, I used to go and visit him. Uncle Len had those "Rashleigh eyes" that would sparkle and shine right back at me! Spending time with him was peaceful and joyous.

Uncle Len's favourite pieces to play were "The Sound of Music" and "The Alley Cat," for which he would improvise the cat sounds from the organ. Leonard had three organs in his home, including a huge console Hammond organ that was built into their living room. Uncle Len was a great encourager for me in becoming a professional musician. He loved to hear me sing. I miss him and his great passion for music in our family.

So there you go. Stemming from the passion of our mutual great-great grandfather on the Rashleigh side, vocal music has now been in the genetic code for five generations. My Rashleigh extended family loved me. They accepted me for who I was as an aspiring artist/musician and singer. I was the first person in this large, talented family who aspired to make a career as a musician.

THE HELMKAY/GARBUTT CONNECTION IN THE FAMILY TREE

My mother, Doreen, has one brother, Norman Helmkay (yes, another "Norman" in the family), who is very mechanical. In collaboration with his colleagues, Norman helped developed the innovative technology resulting in the home computer revolution. As an employee of IBM Canada, Norman and Marion were so blessed to network within this international empire. They have lived, worked, and travelled in Europe, Africa, and the USA. For nearly twenty years, I didn't have much interaction with my uncle until he retired and came home to Canada. Over the last few years since my mom passed away, it's been wonderful to reconnect with Uncle Norman and Aunt Marion, as they both have given me detailed information that I didn't know about the family.

When Grandpa Charlie died in 1972, my Helmkay grandparents had just celebrated their forty-eighth wedding anniversary. My Great-Aunt Mildred Garbutt (formerly Helmkay) had severe arthritis, which eventually took her life in 1975. My Great-Uncle Bob (Mildred's spouse) had been a close family friend to Violet during their teens before Bob met and later married Mildred. As a newlywed couple, Bob and Mildred moved from Toronto to Detroit, Michigan. Uncle Bob had a splendid job working with General Motors as a draftsman. Violet and Bob began to enjoy each other's company in 1976 (after Mildred had passed away). They were married on December 27, 1977. When Uncle Bob married Grandma, his only son, Robert Bruce and his wife, Ruth, became my step uncle and aunt rather than second cousins to me. When my Grandpa Helmkay died, I couldn't just call Uncle Bob "Grandpa," so I later called him "Grandpa Bob." Violet (Helmkay) and Robert (Bob) Garbutt were married for eight happy years.

I asked my mother to edit the historical facts in this chapter. I wanted my stories to be accurate. Mom reminded me about Violet's hidden talent of learning to paint in her seventies. She was very good at it. Violet continued to paint right up to her ninetieth birthday. Her paintings are in several of our family's homes today. One of Grandma's paintings that I adored was of a seaside, which she had specially painted for me. This painting was created from just looking at a postcard. Knowing of my love of the sea, Grandma captured the colours of the waves and the turbulence of the ocean. I loved that painting very much! Somewhere between moving around from house to house I lost that painting, and I would greatly love to have it back.

I enjoy painting but with water colours. I haven't had the time yet to try other media. Maybe I'll follow in the artistic footsteps of the Rashleigh family. A new creative career in retirement!

CHAPTER EIGHT
FOLLOWING WELL-PAVED PATHWAYS OF INTERNATIONAL INFLUENCE

A scripture I love so well is the story of Moses when he and God were discussing his future at the burning bush. Moses basically tells God, "I am not a public speaker. Why don't you use my brother, Aaron?"

> *Then Moses said to the Lord, "Please, Lord, I am not a man of words (eloquent, fluent), neither before nor since You have spoken to Your servant; for I am slow of speech and tongue."* (Exodus 4:10)

God firmly speaks to eighty-year-old Moses and tells him that he is the man of the hour to lead His people out of slavery. When I read this verse, I'm struck especially by the hearing and obeying the voice of God. Like me, Moses had a disability, yet he had to be obedient to follow his destiny in God. I am nobody except that I am teachable and willing to be used of God in sharing His love and His light to all that I encounter. I have been so blessed by many individuals who have made a profound impact on my life. Perhaps it's my outgoing and artistic nature that has opened the doors to be able to work alongside wonderful international artists and humanitarians. This chapter is my way to say "thank you" to these individuals that have enriched my life!

Unlike a train that follows its well-worn route, I didn't always know where I was going, yet I didn't want to get off the track that would take me to where God wanted me to be. At the end of twelfth grade, my only way to escape a lot of the emotional pain was to visualize and dream that I was either on the concert stage or in movies, performing in musicals like my movie/comedic mentors: Lucille Ball, Red Skelton, Danny Kaye, Bob Hope, George Burns, and Gracie Allen. Having studied the personal histories of these great comedians, I made quite a discovery. Most of these individuals were deeply affected in their childhood by some type of abuse or trauma within the family setting. These comedians overcame a lot of their own obstacles as they succeeded in becoming internationally acclaimed entertainers. I can empathize with their efforts! Perhaps this is the reason why to this day I adore these gifted comedians of the golden age of radio and television. Someone once described me as being an old soul of the theatre. Perhaps this statement is true!

In my thirties and forties, I devoured these artists' biographical details, looking for that similar factor in overcoming trauma and staying focused on one's goal. Reading, learning, and growing are my key methods for therapy. This is the way that I try to keep all the negative issues in my life in one compartment. I was determined, despite my own learning disability, that I was going to achieve something outstanding in my life and career. I would use the same determination and passionate energy as my film and television role models used to build their careers and lifetime.

There was something innovative about the 1930–50s movie and television stars and their involvement with pre-production details. Many of them had a creative say in shows/movies written, produced, and recorded for both radio and film as well as early television. To this day,

I love reading about the "backstory" of how these movies and television shows were created and produced.

As I have explained in other chapters, my home life was reasonably stable; however, that wasn't the case with my public and high school emotional experiences. I reached nearly six feet three inches by the time I graduated from high school. Vocal training and performing were my way of coping with all of the negative bullying issues that battered my self-esteem.

When I began my voice lessons at the age of nine, I would watch Rodgers and Hammerstein musicals on television. The first movie musical that I remember watching in the mid-1960s (in black and white television) was *Oklahoma* and *Carrousel* starring Shirley Jones and Gordon McRae. I was mesmerized watching these musicals on television.

Family would try to talk to me while these movies or television programs were on, but I wouldn't respond. I was thinking and studying every detail about each film or television angle or image of the show. In my mind, I mentally recorded each step and camera position. How did they do that? How does a singer do this or that during a dramatic sequence? And so on. Right there and then, I determined that I was going to be a singing-actor like Gordon McRae, my hero!

Perhaps I was drawn to the drama of being both an actor and a singer, such as Julie Andrews, Shirley Jones, Judy Garland, or Barbra Streisand. My male role models, such as Gordon McRae, Gene Kelly, or Fred Astaire, would become a part of my daily vocabulary … as if they were my close friends.

BEING MENTORED BY JUDY GARLAND AND BARBRA STREISAND

During my teen years, watching the varied songs and performances of Judy Garland and Barbra Streisand opened the creative, musical, and emotional desires within me. I began my own research and read biographies and many articles on both Judy and Barbra's career and how they became show business legends. At fourteen to sixteen years of age, I frequented the library and borrowed many LPs, listening to the "Best of Judy and Barbra's" earliest recordings. I listened to both of their vocal stylings and then committed to memory many songs from their vast song catalogues. After completing many hours of research on both artists, I developed my own interpretation of this vocal style from both these iconic voices. Without a doubt, they have both left their imprints on Broadway tunes all the way to the vocal pop music genre.

Video emerged when I reached my twenties. I watched and studied these legends through a deeper microscope—their films. Barbra Streisand's talent and artistry would captivate me! Streisand still is the consummate actress, through her Broadway recordings and later her pop albums. There is no one in the business that can portray the drama of the lyrics in a song better than Barbra Streisand!

Now through the aid of video and the Internet, it's wonderful seeing Barbra recording in the studio. I can visualize how she emphasizes each word, line, or phrasing that she wants to interpret, along with her incredible breath control. Barbra's artistry is nothing short of magic with music. From varied videos of Streisand's recording in the studio, she gives such dramatic performances. It is not surprising to me that even now in the later years of Barbra's career, the world still wants to attend one of her live performances or watch her many world concerts on DVD and/or the Internet.

In 1983 when Barbra recorded "Where is it Written?" from the movie *Yentl*, I felt so attuned to the lyrics in this song that I would listen to it over and over. *Finally*, I said to myself, *someone else understands how I feel in my soul to be an individual artist with so many unfulfilled dreams.* As the lyrics of this song imply, I was constantly being told that I couldn't move into the place that I wanted to be.

Barbra's artistry and her persona of being a singing/actor have mentored me in so many ways in what I call "vocal pop." When I want to try something new, such as experiment with new sounds, or research arrangements of old songs, I still reflect on her style. It's that Streisand touch that I think about in the back of my mind when developing and refining one's own craft regarding this musical genre.

My personal Streisand collection is extensive: LPs, CDs, VHS tapes of TV interviews and such, and a DVD collection of her music, as well as the television specials, her movies, and, of course, the magic ... which is to me Barbra Streisand. When I was sixteen, my family was vacationing and camping in Myrtle Beach, South Carolina. I walked twenty miles (ten miles each way) from our campsite to see and experience Barbra Streisand in the movie *A Star is Born*. I wanted to be the first in my group of artistic friends and chums in drama class to see this movie.

My parents wouldn't drive me from our campsite to the local theatre to see the film, so I walked. And I walked the return trip as well—a total of twenty miles, round trip, in a completely unfamiliar territory and state. Walking back to our tent trailer after the movie in the dark was a frightening experience. I recall that I sang to myself some pop songs to keep myself calm in very unfamiliar surroundings. I was sixteen and I wanted to prove to myself and my parents that when I said I was going to do something, I would follow through with it! I attended the late evening showing and got back to our campsite around 2:00 a.m., much to the relief of my worried parents.

I had many bad blisters on my feet and toes from this walking experience; however, as I grew in my artistic training, something deep inside me told me that this experience was the catalyst proving that I could be very determined and focused on my art. This was the first of many determined steps toward my own professional journey and my aspirations as a future vocal artist, performer, producer, and, later, choral conductor.

I already knew of Garland's outstanding performance in this same character role in the 1954 version of the movie. In the 1970s, I was just starting to appreciate Barbra's vast song catalogue. I was completely mesmerized by Barbra's vocals, her dramatic artistry, and energy within the film as Ester Hoffman in her version of *A Star is Born*.

In the last few years, I have added to my DVD collection Barbra's movies *A Star Is Born* and *Yentl*, with Barbra providing a voice–over commentary about how the movie, scene by scene or in general, was created, produced, and then made.

Completing academic courses in high school and in university was difficult. It was my arts courses of music, drama, and film that I focused on to graduate and receive my BA, plus other degrees. Listening and watching both Garland and Streisand films helped me to understand the music and film industry as well as learn about the Broadway and pop stars of their era.

Having worked in the entertainment industry for over thirty years, I now have networked with musicians, contacts, or even some colleagues and friends, who personally know Barbra Streisand. I am hoping that soon I will have the opportunity to meet Barbra personally and thank her for all that she has meant to me as an artist and mentor for so many years.

As a classically trained singer, I occasionally hear a singer that moves me with incredible technique, vocal dexterity, and repertoire. Then I become hooked on this artist and usually buy all their ongoing discography. What can I say about Celine Dion that hasn't already been said? As a Canadian, I am so proud that we have this amazing French-Canadian hometown girl who is multi-talented and has become one of the world's superstars of our age. Celine has a tremendous heart and spends some of her pre-concert time meeting and greeting disabled children and adults who have physical and/ or mental disabilities.

In August 2008, Elaine and I won tickets to Celine's live World Tour in Toronto. Sponsored by Hamilton's K-LITE FM Radio Station, the tickets were worth over $200 each and included box seats complete with food and beverage service. We had amazing seats, and the view of Celine on stage was incredible; it was truly an moving experience for both of us. Some of my favourite songs that Celine has recorded are: "The Colour of My Love," "River Deep and Mountain High," "All by Myself," "Drove All Night," "Love Can Move Mountains," and Elaine's and my song, "Because You Loved Me."

As a producer/director, I am always fascinated when someone extends the boundaries between art and live stage performance. Celine and her late husband, Rene Angelil, combined with their company, Feeling Productions Inc., have produced the most incredible show from Celine's former five-year engagement in Las Vegas entitled "A New Day." The DVD is spectacular, as the viewer not only gets to watch Celine perform eighteen of her mega pop hits but can see the magic of Dragone's Cirque du Soleil-type choreography. With an incredible troupe of dancers, this double DVD is well worth the price. For every Celine fan like me, it's a must for your collection! I hope soon that Elaine and I will have the opportunity to meet Celine.

When I was working with Orchestra London Canada (OLC) in 1988, I had the opportunity to meet and chat with David Foster, Canada's own international producer, singer/songwriter, and recording impresario. David and I were chatting at a hospital event. At that time, he was on a concert tour singing many of his musical selections that were arranged for orchestra. We were trying to secure some dates when we could work together with OLC; however, that didn't work out. I would love to work with David Foster and his team in the near future!

From the world of artists and celebrities, I also have had the opportunity to meet some outstanding sports heroes. In the mid 1980s, I was introduced to Mr. and Mrs. Hockey themselves, Gordie and Colleen Howe. I knew who Gordie Howe was, but was fascinated with his amazing wife, Colleen. She did most of the talking, and in the later years of his career was Gordie's agent. My brother, Andrew, is a huge hockey fan, as was my dad. I asked Gordie for his autograph for my brother and when I gave it to him, he almost fell through the floor! Here at this London, Ontario hospital benefit were the Howes again, and it was great spending some moments with them. Gordie and Colleen have now passed away, and what a legacy they have both given to the international "hockey communities" and to their family.

One dear friend who I want to acknowledge is Virginia Henderson Caldwell of London, Ontario. In the early 1990s we became close friends from my connection of working with OLC. Virginia is a piano and theory teacher, who in the early years helped me with my theory requirements. Not only is Virginia a great musician, but she is an established visual artist. As a painter, she taught me so much about living one's life as an artist, especially in how one learns to evaluate life from the perspective of the gifts and abilities one has been given. We talked many times about not letting others steal your passion and dreams away, regardless of what the world would tell you to do or how to behave or function as an artist.

Virginia was a valuable mentor to me as I developed my artistic bent. We both share a passion for the artistry of Glenn Gould. Getting together with her to attend different galleries and concerts provided great times of discussion, with her teaching me about the Canadian performing and visual artists' landscape. I grew in knowledge as a young artist/administrator by just spending time with Virginia. As my life evolved, we lost contact with each other until November 2010, when we reconnected. Virginia is one of my oldest and closest friends with whom I'm so glad to be able to share all my joys and sorrows, as well as my recent awards and achievements.

In the fall of 1981, during my prep year working and singing in The Toronto Mendelssohn Youth Choir (TMYC), I decided that I needed weekly voice lessons so that I could gain acceptance to university. I wanted to study with Mr. Paul Massel (now known as Father Paul Massel), who was in great demand as a voice instructor and performer in musical theatre as well as opera from 1980 into the 2000s. Paul taught me vocal techniques in belle canto style (beautiful singing technique that applies to the distinctive styles of art song), opera, and musical theatre. I gained much knowledge and interpretation of many vocal stylings of repertoire from Paul's teaching and mentoring techniques.

A STUDENT SINGER'S PERSONAL ANGST

In the spring 1983, I performed a classical half recital with a female singer from the studio of my first vocal professor at the Faculty of Music. When I was at UWO, I was told that no one ever performed a vocal recital in their first year. I was told that first-year students have many studies and activities to keep them busy, and it was generally frowned upon to do this concert. I wanted to gain the experience of singing in this small yet effective concert hall and performing my soon- to-be jury pieces. I would be judged by the vocal faculty for my first year-set of juries before going into the second year of my music degree.

The final grade for my first year at Western would determine if I would be placed in the music education or in the vocal performance divisions of my degree program. Mary Morrison Friedman was on this jury, and she gave me the best mark that I received from a faculty member, which was

78 per cent for my efforts. I have never forgotten her comments or this grade to this day.

In 1984, my second year at the Faculty of Music, I studied and was in the vocal studio of Professor Martin Chambers, a tenor soloist who was a brilliant singing character actor with the Canadian Opera Company, then under the Artistic Director leadership of Lofti Mansouri. Martin was also my opera workshop vocal professor. I learned many amazing techniques from him on preparation of pre-to post-vocal production, stage and performance techniques, and most importantly, how to research and develop a character role. We also learned a great deal from this class about movement relative to the stage.

One of the sessions was on how to move in a nearly dark or barely lit stage. As singing actors, we were asked to move to where we thought centre stage was located. In an almost blacked-out stage environment, I was the only one of my classmates that got it right. I was standing centre stage! I always remember that experience, and I always feel so at home in the theatre, on or off stage.

While in this opera study course and during my Faculty of Singers choral ensemble rehearsals, I had the wonderful opportunity to become good friends with Canadian and international soprano, Adrianne Pieczonka, O.C. As part of our preparation, our opera class could only perform excerpts from Mozart's *The Marriage of Figaro* in English instead of Italian. Neither did we have an orchestra or full stage lighting in this production. We performed this opera in a "opera-in-concert version" with only piano accompaniment.

I performed the baritone role of Count Almaviva with Adrianne as the countess and another soprano in our class as Susanna performing the duet of number 13 in the opera, "Susanna or via sortie!" I was not very pleased with my own performance, as, due to nerves, I missed a cue with the recitative, and it threw me off during our duet and then trio; however, we continued.

Adrianne had that vocal sparkle and incredible stage presence when she was in the solo spot. As I watched her perform the role of the countess, I knew that of all my vocal friends at Western, Adrianne would be the one who would become the next Marilyn Horne of our generation of singers. Early on in Adrianne's career, she was a mezzo soprano, and as she matured, Adrianne became a coloratura soprano. Boy, was I right on the money! We've been great friends since then, and when it's accessible for both of our schedules, we have regular coffee meetings in Toronto. I am so pleased by Adrianne's success, now one of our own Canadian International Divas of the twenty-first century.

The Toronto Mendelssohn Choir offices were at Roy Thomson Hall (RTH). In 2001, I was very fortunate on behalf of RTH to give a bouquet of flowers to Adrianne at her first RTH vocal recital. She was very well received by her Toronto fans! Elaine and I enjoyed catching up with Adrianne, her family, and friends backstage. In 2007, Adrianne Pieczonka, O.C. was awarded the Order of Canada for her outstanding achievements as musical ambassador of Canada's opera and vocal music genre. Today, the world at large has many opportunities to interact with my dear friend Adrianne and her amazing vocal and performance talents.

Spending some great "backstage" time with Adrianne Pieczonka and Elaine in 2001 (ECG Photo Collection)

MEETING TWO OF CANADA'S NATIONAL ARTISTIC TREASURES

During my final year at Western in 1984, I developed two wonderful and lifelong friendships with Nicholas Goldschmidt, C.C. and Maureen Forrester, C.C. Both are Canadian icons in performance and vocal music. Here I was at twenty-four years of age connecting with these two legends known and loved in both the Canadian classical and international music circles.

"Niki" (as everyone close to him was instructed to call him) and I were introduced in 1984 when he came to Western to give a lecture on opera and attend a master class with Maureen Forrester. At this time, he announced his upcoming International Choral Festival. It would be the first year that Niki and his board of directors would launch his successful choral festivals in Toronto for three non-consecutive years. These choral festivals contained an amazing international cast of vocal talent that featured some unique choral programming with once in a lifetime memorable vocal and choral performances.

I wanted to be involved in these choral events and hopefully gain some further arts administration skills. Despite my best efforts, I could not get my foot in the door; however, I did succeed in building a relationship with Niki. After the lecture, I acted as his liaison with the faculty, and this introduction and friendship to him was the beginning of a twenty-year friendship and connection with one of Canada's and the world's greatest classical and opera producers.

Niki's philosophy from the beginning of his fifty-plus year performance career was that the lead vocal roles for his productions would first be given to Canadian talent, either up-and-coming or seasoned. His Canadian Artist First mandate was a very firm objective for him, as he worked with many boards of directors throughout his artistic endeavours. Niki's firm directive of showcasing Canadian artists has advanced the careers of many known national treasures in our country. From coast to coast he founded music festivals, promoted and showcased Canadian composers, and produced operas and choral music as well as vocal music recitals.

Nicholas Goldschmidt was also one of the original founders of the Canadian Opera Company. I encourage you to do your own research via the Internet on the outstanding life and career of Nicholas Goldschmidt. It was always such a joy meeting up with Niki and his wonderful wife, Shelagh, at various choral concerts or opera performances. Being able to chat with both and get Niki's feedback on a performance was a real treat. This professional friendship grew throughout the years, and Niki became a valuable contact for me. From time to time as a young, maturing choral arts administrator, I was given wonderful opportunities to seek his advice.

In 2003, I was studying for my Post-Graduate Certificate at Humber College, Toronto, in the Fundraising and Volunteer Management program. I called Niki for some advice and feedback on a fundraising question. He was then in his mid-nineties. I told him that upon graduation from the course, I wanted to find a middle development officer position in a good arts organization and use all my newly developed skills to the best of my ability. At the age of ninety-four, Niki said:

> "I have watched you over these years, and if I am able to launch another music or choral festival, I would love to have you on my board of directors, as you have the right passion and now skills to be a great asset for my board and their interests. My only problem is that over the years I have worn out my friends and associates from my previous festivals; however, if I was up to it, I would welcome you warmly to this team of seasoned professionals."

I was deeply honoured by his comments and I told him so. Sadly, early in February of 2004, having just turned ninety-five, Niki passed away. He left an incredible arts legacy and a deep void within the Canadian and international arts community that can never be replaced!

After Niki's passing, the late Shelagh (Fraser) Goldschmidt became a dear friend to me. She lived to be 109 years old and passed away in her almost 110th year in 2016. Shelagh was a wealth of knowledge about the Canadian and Toronto arts scene from its beginning in the 1940s to the 1990s. I enjoyed hearing her stories and memories, as both Shelagh and Niki were founding members of the National Ballet of Canada and the Canadian Opera Company, which all began (building the initial committees) right there in their living room in Toronto. Shelagh acted as hostess in their homes in Toronto and Vancouver. She entertained Niki's many friends in Canada's, as well as the world's, stage of artists, producers, and directors who participated in Niki's many projects and festivals. Consequently, at that same first meeting of Nicholas Goldschmidt at the University of Western Ontario, I was introduced to Canadian and internationally-renown Maureen Forrester, contralto. Niki and Maureen were old friends and had worked together on many concerts, operas, and projects.

A MEMORABLE MOMENT—MAUREEN FORRESTER'S MASTER CLASS

In the early 1980s, Maureen had become the chairman of the Canada Council and was at UWO giving an incredible master class to the vocal students and faculty. Known as "Madame Mahler" for her amazing interpretation of Mahler's vocal music, she was warm and generous and so down-to-earth. Maureen made each student feel important with the vocal pieces they chose to sing to her. When I was then introduced to her, I found Maureen to be warm and very personable.

During the Master class with Maureen in 1984, she was firm yet gracious with the young singers. Maureen coached them along, accepting them right where they were in their young careers and applauding them when they took risks. Some singers perhaps didn't make the best choices vocally, as some were unable to obtain the right vowel or colour sound that Maureen was looking for at that moment; however, she let the young singers perform and then corrected tiny things here and there, as it should be in a good master class environment.

It was exciting being in the audience and listening to how Maureen worked with each student. Just by tweaking a few problems or clarifying one's diction, they immediately improved in their presentation. This master class was such a treat! I have recently been to other master classes with other internationally known divas who seem to bully their young students ... but not Maureen. Always with grace, class, and humour she instructed these singers to perform at their best. No wonder young singers and musicians would flock to Maureen like bees to nectar.

MAUREEN AND ME ON HER FAVOURITE PIECE, "VERDI'S REQUIEM"
In 1988, as part of the London Pro Musica (LPM) choral ensemble, I had the opportunity to get to know Maureen personally and work with her as one of our featured soloists in "Verdi's Requiem." This was a media junket which consisted of interviews with Maureen, LPM, and the Kitchener Philharmonic Choir (now known as the Grand Philharmonic Choir), under the joint direction of Howard Dyck, Music Director for both choirs. These indeed were my apprenticeship years, and oh what fun there were!

As LPM's volunteer publicity director, I was in perfect position to gain much practical experience while promoting these amazing artists and these two choirs. It was truly a blessing to work and interact with Maureen on these media interviews. What a pro she was on selling and promoting the show! In Kitchener, as we both were starving after the press junket, Maureen took me out to dinner and we became friends. During the dinner, Maureen gave me some very important advice on maintaining one's career and especially in staying in touch with one's family while on the road. This special "chat" with Maureen, and her advice, is something that I have never forgotten!

The wrap-up celebration party for the "Verdi Requiem" in London of April 1987 was open to all LPM members and our special artists. Maureen entertained us all with her funny and witty jokes and antidotes. She generously shared her memories and stories of international concerts or performing experiences throughout the world. Her stories were priceless. Maureen could bring us close to tears with laughter and the context of the story, especially if she was speaking in her family's Scottish accent. Maureen would receive questions from the media or other singers as to her international career. Always the lady, she would not speak about her personal music making memories regarding working with individual and celebrity conductors. Tactfully, she kept these experiences to herself.

During the cast party, Maureen shared one of her priceless stories. On a warm mid-April, Easter Saturday evening, the other vocal soloists were drinking water from their cups placed near their seats. Maureen didn't drink any water on stage during the entire performance. Afterwards, she was asked how she survived. She said, "Listen, I was the oldest singer on the stage, and if I had accidently kicked the cup, they would have been saying that the old lady can't hold her bladder and look what happened. I didn't want to risk the embarrassment!" That was a typical quick witted and humorous comment that would leave Maureen's audience in stitches.

Whenever Maureen was performing in Toronto or in London, Ontario, I would find my way backstage after a show. She would greet me and want to hear all the news of what I was doing musically or professionally at that time of my life.

Sadly, toward the end of a brilliant career in the late 1990s, Maureen was diagnosed with dementia and later Alzheimer's disease. She was one of our national and international treasures. Maureen was passionate about music and the arts, and of course so well connected within the global arts community. Sadly, Maureen would lose that bubbling belle-of-the-ball personality, and the Canadian and world arts community would grieve the loss of another artist to this debilitating disease.

In the fall of 2006, the Canadian Opera Company (COC) honoured both Nicholas Goldschmidt and Maureen Forrester with entry into the COC Luminaries Gallery, hosted by the late Richard Bradshaw. Other outstanding vocal national treasures, such as the late Jon Vickers and Lofti Mansouri, were also honoured for their contribution of vocal talent to the Canadian Opera Company and its audiences. As a guest of Shelagh Goldschmidt, I had a wonderful evening at this COC event. Seeing both these dear friends recognized for their rightful place in Canadian vocal and operatic history was immensely satisfying.

On June 16, 2010, at the age of seventy-nine, my friend and mentor passed away. Maureen will always have a special place in my heart. I will always remember her warm hugs and smiles when we would reconnect during my early years as an arts manager/chorister.

Recently, while going through some of my mom's 1950s black and white photographs, I came to understand why many people told her that she resembled Maureen Forrester. The similarity was in the very same way my mom cocked her head in posing for pictures. Losing both my mom and Maureen in the same year was very difficult for me. They were both seventy-nine. Thank goodness for the Internet providing all of us opportunity to watch and listen to Maureen's memorable performances, recordings, and concerts with her marvellous, rich contralto voice. She will never be forgotten!

RELATIONSHIP BUILDING WITH YOUR VOCAL TEACHER OR COACH

As important as role models are for the aspiring musical artist, the relationship with one's vocal teacher or coach is vital. It's critical that a singer be on the same wavelength as their instructor. It is especially important to be able to communicate when unsure of one's ability. The human voice is not an instrument that you can pick up and play or practice on a whim, which is why you hear so many stories about singers' emotions or their personal traumas. If one is having a difficult day emotionally and vocally, it will be unpleasantly evident and carry through into the rehearsal and even the concert.

Martin Chambers and I didn't always see eye-to-eye on my vocal interpretation. At the time, the timbre of my baritone vocal sound wasn't fully developed. Going through yet another awkward stage, I lacked confidence in my own performing abilities. When I was around him, I felt inadequate when I wasn't understanding all that he was trying to teach me about the production of my sound. Again, I faced yet another indication of ADHD—not grasping verbal instructions when I was nervous or unsure of myself.

I was dealing with my own emotional and personal problems at that time. I assume that all music students worry about one's natural abilities, self-esteem, and the "Will I be able to make it as a professional singer and musician?" syndrome. I recall that I was deeply concerned about my studies, my grades, and being accepted into either the vocal performance or music education degree as my major. As a vocal performance major at UWO, you had to have at least a 75 per cent average to be considered for the degree program. This was a percentage I did not have.

My inability to sing in different languages was also a problem. Being able to sing and speak other languages was a requisite, and I just didn't have the extra resources or time to take further study in these courses. Had I known about my learning disability and the resulting difficulty with memorization, this would have given me some relief. Instead, I beat myself up mentally. Why couldn't I retain all this information?

I think that my ADHD issues were really at my ultimate stress levels. With so many problems with my academics, I was constantly on edge. I felt so inadequate and at times I felt that I was drowning with all the work that I couldn't always keep up or stay ahead of myself, especially for due dates of my written academic papers. Along with trauma, I was having problems with learning to sing in different languages and in memorizing these lyrics for future juries.

I remember talking to Adrianne about this. In her senior years at Western, she was studying Russian. Adrianne wanted to be prepared for the Russian repertoire that many opera roles required at the University of Toronto's Opera School. I knew that I couldn't compete in this arena. Other young singers were preparing themselves as opera soloists, planning their careers by taking additional languages or acting courses.

The second problem I faced was my performance stance. Despite the apparent simplicity of simply standing erect without hunching, leaning, tensing, or over-arching one's spine, even seasoned professionals with years of singing experience can sense points of unevenness or over-tension. When singing on stage, it's not correct to place one foot behind the other. One deceptively simple exercise in attaining what singers call a neutral posture is to imagine the spine lengthening as one stands. I am already a tall singer and was convinced that I couldn't stand properly without looking like a scarecrow. These emotional and physical problems were draining on me during my solo performance opportunities. Martin worked with me on my stance, which at first felt very uncomfortable.

Why couldn't I sing naturally despite how I was standing? Couldn't I simply let my God-given vocal sound come out while I was performing? Finally, I did develop a comfortable stance that has now become as much a part of me and as natural as breathing.

One late Friday afternoon in 1984, toward the end of the school term, Martin and I talked about my future aspirations as a professional opera singer. He told me flat out that he didn't think I would make it. I felt like the sandbags suspended overhead in the wings of a theatre dropped squarely on my head! I was devastated! I was very interested in arts administration and had some success at the faculty level, which had attracted interest and encouragement from others. Martin thought that this would be a productive career choice for me, and I could pursue singing as a part-time career. Choosing arts administration as a career would be less stressful than having to forge on, hoping to develop a vocal career.

At first I was physically and emotionally crushed by Martin bursting my balloon; however, as the years have passed, I realize that Martin's wise counsel saved me many more years of pain. I developed my energies and my abilities on becoming a professional arts administrator as well as being chorister and now music director and conductor.

Barbra Streisand, in an interview, referred to thanking those teachers that said no to you and your talent at a time in your student life. So thank you, Martin Chambers, for your honesty and wise counsel. I am so glad that you steered me onto the right career path that has blessed my life in so many ways!

CHAPTER NINE
THE MAGICAL LAND OF "TANGLEWOOD"

After my first full season with the Toronto Mendelssohn Youth Choir (TMYC), I auditioned for the Ontario Youth Choir during the early spring of 1981. Sadly, I was not accepted, yet for some reason my application was passed on to Leonard Atherton, the music director of the Young Artist Vocal Program (YAVP) of the Boston University Tanglewood Institute (BUTI) in Lenox, Massachusetts. Leonard Atherton, an English conductor, was the artistic director of Chorus Niagara. Years later, this position would be filled by Robert Cooper, my friend and mentor.

In the choral program and office of BUTI, there was a need for more men to join the chorus, so the Institute was willing to offer me a scholarship to be a part of this summer program. All I needed to do was send them an audition tape so that they could hear my vocal range. If I was accepted into the program, I would then need to arrange for my own transportation to Tanglewood.

Since graduating from Grade Twelve in 1980, I had tried switching into a different career, such as real estate. However, when the opportunity to possibly attend Tanglewood opened, I sensed that this was God's direction providing me with this choral apprentice program. Technically, I qualified for being in this vocal program, as I had not entered university or college. Once again, I was three years older than most of my classmates. I was a young, inexperienced Canadian baritone singer with a golden-ticket experience (and scholarship) moving toward my musical dreams and aspirations. I would connect with some of the world's finest musicians and artists by just being involved in the BUTI Program.

In discussing this opportunity with my parents, they agreed to pay half of my fees to Tanglewood on the condition that I could raise the other half. The entire summer program cost me less than $5,000, and it was worth every penny! I was very determined that I wasn't going to miss this musical experience! I am extremely proud to be an alumnus of the YAVP, Class of 1981.

I knew nothing of the Tanglewood's eight-week summer music and educational program with its international legendary performance status. I spent many hours doing my research on what I could expect. One could listen to almost every style of music, including selections from operas, right there. When I was twenty-one, still unsure of where I wanted to go to college or university and what I wanted to do with my life, the only thing I knew for certain was that my career would involve music and the arts.

Just before I left Hamilton for the summer, I was working two jobs— one at the Hamilton Public Library on the Arts floor, and one working night shifts as a security guard at one of the biggest and most prestigious office towers in downtown Hamilton. I would work my night shift at the security job and then in the morning I would walk over to the library between 7:00 or 7:30 a.m. With special arrangements with the library security staff, I would then crash in a bed in the nurse's station.

I would wake up with an alarm clock and get up mid-morning, rather groggy from only four or five hours of sleep. Then I would work my four to five hour part-time shift at the library from the afternoon until early evening. Finally, I would stagger to catch the bus to Westdale and connect with my dad for the drive home. After that I'd collapse on my bed and sleep well into the next day. Could I work that kind of schedule now? Not on your life! The things that we do for our art as young people!

When I finally mailed all the paperwork and demo tape to BUTI, I was already learning how to self-promote, publicize, and fundraise while gaining awareness for my summer program. I needed to raise $2,500 to match the financial commitment of my parents. To that end, I had my first newspaper interview. I also began to learn how to research Hamilton-based corporations, sponsors, and individuals. Learning these initial steps was all about building relationships.

Within six weeks I had raised around $1,500–$2,000. My own Baptist Convention gave me $500 through the Hymnal Committee with the condition that I would write an article on my choral experiences and the music that we performed. Being involved with BUTI was my initial beginning in arts management and fundraising. I enjoyed the experience so much! Maybe it would be a full-time career in the future.

Then it all crashed. After doing all this work, I was told that "due to my age" I couldn't be accepted into YAVP, as the program was for youth up to the age of eighteen. Speaking on the phone to the program administrator, I reasoned with him that I had raised all the money and had gained a lot of public support to attend Tanglewood. He agreed for me to be accepted into the program; however, I didn't know until the end of that summer that I wasn't fully registered into the BUTI program, nor was I listed or included in the official records as "alumni of the program" until 2006.

At the end of the summer, I learned from some of the program staff that they all thought that I was one of this administrator's "boyfriends." This individual was known for having an interest in young men. He had accepted my money; however, he didn't inform the faculty or BUTI about how old I was or what I was doing in this program. Looking back, I can see that God was protecting me and keeping me just under the radar while allowing me to experience an amazing time of friendship, music making, and vocal and choral development.

I could only afford to travel by bus from Hamilton to Lenox, Massachusetts. Knowing that I would be the oldest chorister in the program didn't bother me all. I knew that God had made a space for me in this program, and I was there for His specific purpose.

MEETING MY LIFELONG FRIEND, ALPHA

Once I arrived and registered, I settled into my assigned room. Just as I was coming to the dining hall, I met Alpha Omega (Gonzales) Cruiz-Lopez from Houston, Texas. She was majoring in the Harp Program. Both feeling overwhelmed, we decided to stick together and discovered that we had a lot in common. We were both Baptist youths. Alpha was accompanied by her mother, whom I later called "Momma Gonzalez," and her brother, Gerry. They returned to Houston after Alpha was settled.

Due to a national Canadian mail strike, I didn't get many letters from home. To send me occasional care packages letters and a money order, my parents would have to drive an hour to the border. Once Momma Gonzalez heard that I wasn't receiving mail, she would write to me as faithfully as she did Alpha. Until we both got comfortable with our individual schedules, Alpha and I sat together for meals and attended many concerts together.

My "Magical Summer at Tanglewood" in 1981, singing and participating in the Young Artist Vocal Program (YAVP) (Whitestone Photo Collection)

One memory I recall is of the beautiful music played by harp students at the end of the day. All students had been working hard on practicing, music theory lessons, or homework. The melodious sounds would ring throughout the big old mansion, which had been converted into dormitories. In that special old mansion, known today as Groton Place, all the students would stand or gather around the hallway as well as the staircase. Today, thirty-five years later, I am still in regular contact with my friend Alpha and her family.

THE NUTS AND BOLTS OF THE BUTI VOCAL PROGRAM

Once into the summer program, we performed with excellent musicians, singers, vocal coaches, and young conductors. Now as alumni, many of us have graced the stages of the Boston Symphony Orchestra (BSO), Boston University (BU), and Boston Conservatory of Music, as well as other international orchestras. Our alumni are now lawyers, doctors, and professors, as well as performing artists … with even a Broadway composer from our distinguished group!

In the pioneering days of the YAVP, there was only one chorus rehearsal and one vocal lesson per week. To alleviate boredom, the vocal summer students were entertained by a sword swallower. Boring!

Our music director, Leonard Atherton, introduced the rotation of many lectures. Utilizing guest artists already on the Tanglewood grounds for master classes and voice production seminars improved the program. They offered lectures on arts management, building one's vocal career, and the Alexander Technique.

We had many opportunities to perform within the churches or private homes of various patrons in our certain vocal ensembles, quartets, or smaller choirs. One wealthy individual invited the entire YAVP chorus to his home. The entrance to his home reminded me of Bruce Wayne's (Batman's) mansion. During the evening, we performed for this gentleman and his family and then watched the first beta film of *Star Wars*. In 1981, this technology was truly unique, as home video had yet to become popularized.

The YAVP of almost sixty singers and staff was divided into different ensembles, madrigal groups, quartets, and smaller choruses.

The vocal program entailed performing two large works plus one newly commissioned work. Through an amazing lecture, we were introduced to the little-known female composer, Fanny Mendelssohn. She composed 466 pieces of music, including a piano trio and several solo piano pieces and songs. Several of her songs were originally published under her brother Felix's name in his Opus 8 and 9 collections.

We attended a vocal Master class with the legendary soprano Phyllis Curtin, who has trained many graduate students. We were so fortunate to have a lecture and Master class from Canadian and international contralto Catherine Robbins, as well as a lecture from Sir Andrew Davis (former artistic director of the Toronto Symphony Orchestra). Sir Andrew spoke on Haydn's "Missa Solemnis" that we would be performing during our final concert. In addition, each vocal student had a private music lesson each week. I studied with Miss Mary Davenport, the legendary vocal artist and teacher for the summer.

THE HANDSHAKE THAT CHANGED MY LIFE

As students from YAVP, we were invited to participate as the audience for Leonard Bernstein's "Divertimento for Orchestra," a newly commissioned work for the BSO's one hundredth Birthday. "Lenny" conducted the Young Artist Instrumental Program (YAIP) of this work after the premiere. Our class performed Bernstein's "Chichester Psalms" at the end of the summer.

Without a doubt, my experiences of meeting, shaking hands, and chatting with Leonard Bernstein were monumental for me. We chatted about my initial "Chichester Psalms" Toronto performance. I shared with him how Robert Cooper, our TMYC conductor (when we performed this work), had worked very hard on the second movement and in getting the emotional response of the men's voices to react in anger, as was written in the score, while singing in Hebrew. "Lenny" listened and smiled as I shared my memoires with him about performing this special and sacred choral work.

You can read all about this experience for yourself in an article I wrote concerning my meeting and future "passion for Bernstein." It was my first published international article included in *Preludes, Fugues and*

Riff's Fall/Winter edition in 2002, published by the Leonard Bernstein Foundation.

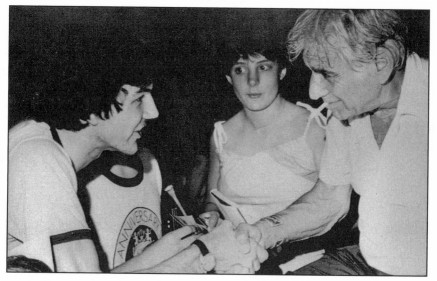

Shaking hands with the legendary musician, composer, and conductor, Leonard Bernstein, at Tanglewood in 1981 (Whitestone Photo)

BEGINNING A LONG-LASTING FRIENDSHIP WITH ELLEN RESNICK AND OTHERS

Another special friendship that has lasted for thirty-five years is with Ellen Resnick. Ellen, an alto, bunked with soprano Martha Schuchard and violinist, Julie Johnson of the YAIP. As I got to know these ladies, a big brother relationship was formed among the four of us. Ellen was the life of the party, and she could tell us all types of stories about her Jewish family and her life experiences. These stories would keep us all in stitches. One weekend Ellen invited six of us to spend a weekend with her at her parents' home in Boston. We had an amazing time!

MEETING THE "THIRD MRS. ROCKWELL"

Another significant adventure with Ellen Resnick happened in Stockbridge, MA, just outside the Norman Rockwell Museum. We had been rehearsing in the local Anglican church in the village on a Saturday. I wanted to see the Rockwell Museum, which was then located just across the street.

Norman Rockwell had just died in 1978. One of the museum aides provided a map and information to visit the homestead. It was not far away. I had been reading the book *A Rockwell Portrait*, written by Donald Walton. Later I would hear that his was a not a good biography.

Leaving the museum, Ellen joined me for the short walk to investigate the home of this great American painter. After looking around the Rockwell property, I wanted to see for myself Norman's private studio and hopefully take a picture of it. Within minutes of us snooping around on the property, a dear woman came out of the building and confirmed that we were at the right place. Thinking that she could be the maid, I told her that I was a Canadian, that this was my first trip to Stockbridge, and that I was a great fan. We didn't know it until a little later into our conversation that we were speaking to the third Mrs. Rockwell, Mrs. Molly (Punderson) Rockwell. Originally a school teacher in the village, she had married Norman in 1961. Mrs. Rockwell invited us into her home. Needless to say, we were gob smacked!

As we walked into the Rockwell home, I couldn't believe my eyes. Original Rockwell paintings were displayed. Here were all the familiar faces and characters of Norman's family, framed and placed on the walls. The originals are now worth millions of dollars.

Mrs. Rockwell was very kind to us and the perfect hostess. We told her that we were involved with the YAVP program at Tanglewood and that I had also been reading Walton's biography. Right away, Mrs. Rockwell told me that she didn't approve of this author. She handed me a typed list of books which she determined I should read. I thanked Mrs. Rockwell for this list. To think that I had been invited into the home of one of my favourite American artists. To this day, I still have that piece of paper in my Tanglewood collection of memorabilia.

WATCHING THE ROYAL WEDDING ON TV IN LENOX, MA

Ellen Resnick and I made an interesting looking pair of friends. Despite our age and height differences, we discovered that we had similar interests. I discovered that she had relatives in Ottawa and that she had been to Canada a few times. I told Ellen about my love and passion for the British Royal Family and of my British heritage.

The summer of 1981 was the date of a major event for all royalists across the globe. Prince Charles and Lady Diana Spencer were about to be married on July 28th, and I was going to be in the States! There was no question. I had to watch this Royal wedding! Where would we watch this Royal television event? Knowing that there was a time difference, we'd need to get up between 4:30–5:00 a.m. Ellen said that she would accompany me. Getting up early, we walked into the centre of town. Nothing was open! I thought, *Am I the only British/Canadian foreigner that wants to see this Royal wedding?*

Walking back to our dormitory, we spotted the local fire department station. To our delight, we discovered that their second-floor lounge housed a television set. Thank the Lord! We got permission from the crew to watch their set. After explaining about my Canadian heritage, the men on duty agreed for us to watch the wedding. No one even bothered us for the next four hours. The hospitable fireman even served us tea beverages. With Ellen by my side, we watched the wedding, and I acted as commentator.

We both "oohed" and "ahhed" at all the festivities and the music and choral selections conducted by Sir David Willcocks. We commented over the lavish details of Diana's wedding dress. Returning around 8:30 a.m., we explained to our classmates that we had gotten up hours before and found this place to watch the wedding. I was one very happy camper! Together we had created a very special memory! I keep a *Boston Globe* newspaper clipping of the Royal Wedding in my Royal collection.

THE PASSING OF LEONARD BERNSTEIN

In 1990, along with the rest of the world, I mourned the loss of Leonard Bernstein. His life and career, punctuated by those few serendipitous moments that I had with him personally, made a deep impression on me. In January 2001, I reconnected with my mentor, Robert Cooper, as I became the TMYC's choir manager. Robert knew of my interest in Bernstein, so he showed me a new magazine, *Preludes, Fugues and Riffs*, published by The Leonard Bernstein Society of New York.

As I read this periodical, I thought to myself, *Perhaps the Foundation might be interested in my story as to how I met Leonard Bernstein.* I then submitted my article to the Bernstein Society to see if they were interested. Robert Cooper assisted me with the editing of the article so that if flowed smoothly with my many personal and academic thoughts. "The Handshake That Changed My Life," was published in *Preludes, Fugues and Riffs* Fall/Winter edition, 2002. The article can still be found at the following link: http://www.leonardbernstein.com/newsletter_past.htm

RECONNECTING WITH MY TANGLEWOOD FRIENDS

In July 2006, BUTI celebrated its fortieth anniversary. Only a handful of our alumni could attend the celebrations. Sadly, I couldn't afford the time to go. I volunteered to use the Internet to research and help Zenobia Perry, our class archivist, build a current list of our alumni for BUTI's fortieth anniversary. It was wonderful reconnecting with fifty-five classmates and former coaches after twenty-six years. Without the Internet and email, this reconnection would not have happened.

COMING HOME TO TANGLEWOOD

In August 2015, twenty-five of us YAVP re-united for a reunion weekend at Tanglewood as we toured our former summer residence, Grotton Place, and had our beloved Leonard Atherton conduct us, once more, singing some of our choral repertoire that we sang that precious summer thirty-four years ago. We once again had a "huge feast and party on the lawn" under our favourite maple tree, where we gathered to relax, eat some scrumptious picnic foods, and enjoy the magical music on many summer evenings in 1981. We once again listened to the wonderful artistry and repertoire of the Boston Symphony Orchestra (BSO).

For me, being back at Tanglewood was a sense of "coming home" as I walked the grounds, taking in the sights and smells of this magical land that was such a blessing for me, growing and maturing as a musician, vocalist, and choral enthusiast. I loved being around these cherished alumni and catching up on everyone's lives, careers, and families since we all were youth at this amazing place during that wonderful summer of 1981. We all came "full circle back to our roots" in this magical land we all call "home" at Tanglewood in Lennox, MA.

"Salt of the Earth"

Written as the theme song for Baptist Youth Encounter 1984
Words and music by W. Ian Walker

CHORUS

Lord, show us how to be your salt upon the
earth;
May every corner be touched by your Spirit and
Word.
Teach us to spread the news that Christ is alive
and well,
So that others may know of His saving grace.
It's hard in this world to show the love of Christ
in daily life;
No matter the cause, it's hard to share His love.
As Jesus reminds us, we are to be salt upon the
earth,
So we must spread His special light to everyone.

CHORUS

Jesus calls us to share the good news, near and
far;
His call is so simple, so plain to hear.
If you'll be my witness unto me, where're you'll
be,
My Father in Heaven will praise your deeds,

CHORUS

CHAPTER TEN
CHORAL AND ARTS MANAGEMENT—FROM
APPRENTICESHIP TO SKILLS

After my Tanglewood experience, I just couldn't stay in Dundas, Ontario. I was twenty-one (wanting to be independent), and my spirit and soul were beckoning me to explore living in Toronto. I enjoyed boarding and living in "the Beaches of Toronto" from September 1981 until August 1982.

I also explored Ontario-based universities. My goal was to major in vocal music with a minor in journalism. My first and only choice was The University of Western Ontario (now known as Western). Having only my high school diploma, I knew that I would need to do well academically in my pre-university courses at the University of Toronto. Never mind that in the early 1980s, students with learning disabilities weren't even considered for a degree program at any university.

As I was preparing to leave Dundas and move to Toronto, my parents found me a place to stay through their Baptist church network. I boarded with two families that year. I found a full-time job as a shipping/receiving clerk at The Children's Bookstore, owned and operated by the late Judy and Hy Sarick (formerly in Mirvish Village at Bloor and Bathurst, Toronto). In the 1980s, the Saricks' bookstore had an international appeal. Their store carried all the most current children's recordings and books. Due to the reputation of the store, their unique and thorough inventory was preferred for private collections, schools, and libraries all over Canada and the USA.

Right there in the bookstore would be concerts featuring artists such as Sharon, Lois, and Bram; Raffi; and Fred Penner. Who could have known that these Canadian children's artists would develop such an international following? In the record department, you could find some golden oldies with many folk groups from the 1950s right up to whomever was currently popular in folk music. I couldn't have asked for a better job!

As of the spring of 2018, this entire block has been pulled down to prepare for another major condo development in Toronto. Honest Ed's Warehouse and Mirvish Village are also gone now. So happy that I've documented this wonderful experience of working in this area of Toronto in my memoirs.

APPRENTICESHIP: BUILDING MY CHORAL MANAGEMENT SKILLS FOR THE FUTURE

While working in the bookstore by day, once a week I could continue singing and performing with the Toronto Mendelssohn Youth Choir (TMYC) under Robert Cooper's direction. Since I was now living and working in Toronto, I could join the choir executive and become an assistant to the choir manager, Kathryn Brown.

For that year's upcoming Youth Choirs in Concert (YCIC) event, I became assistant to the chairman. This management experience gave me many valuable hands-on skills in both choral management and administration. Dr. James Wood was Chairman of the Board and of the TMYC Parents' Committee. It was at his request that I became his assistant for this conference. From this executive position, I become the liaison to all the high school conductors and their youth choirs. These two contacts would prove to be important mentors.

Sadly, in June 2008, James Wood passed away in his eightieth year. He was an amazing mentor. Jim believed in me and in my talents and aspirations, and he was always so supportive. His daughter, Seana-Lee Wood, remains one of my closest friends from my TMYC years. Seana-Lee continues the musical legacy for the Wood family.

Working on the choral youth choir project that year, I could let all my fears and negative attitudes and self-esteem issues fall to the wayside. When you are a rookie in the arts, your experience is gained by participating in one concert or production to another—commonly referred to as "paying your dues." I proved to myself and to my peers that I had the right stuff!

In the spring of 1982, while in performance, I gained a very valuable lesson about coping under stressful conditions in what we call choral "train wrecks or muddles." My personal example concerns when a choir gets ahead of the conductor and there is a momentary breakdown in communication between conductor and choir. TMYC was asked to host a premiere event/ weekend and invited other high school choirs from across the province of Ontario. This choral weekend was a wonderful way to participate in the YCIC inaugural. The event has grown, and in later years the conference has been renamed Kaggik, the Inuit peoples' term for "meeting place."

TMYC was given many opportunities to perform with the late Dr. Elmer Iseler, former artistic director and conductor of the Toronto Mendelssohn Choir (TMC). Elmer was asked to be the guest conductor for this inaugural choral conference. Robert Cooper had rehearsed and prepared TMYC members for this combined mass choral work.

All five choirs were to perform this final piece as the finale for the choral weekend. There were difficult rhythmic passages in the music, so it was imperative to watch both the music score and the conductor for the cues of the piece. During the rehearsal period, Dr. Iseler was patient, working with the combined youth choirs in forming a strong, unified chorus. For this rehearsal, he maintained a consistent beat pattern to his conducting. During the actual concert, Dr. Iseler entered the performance moment and became very expressive in his conducting. So animated were his movements, it became difficult to determine where his down beat was!

The guest youth choirs were totally confused. Right in the middle of the performance, they stopped singing! This silence could have been a total "train wreck." The more experienced TMYC members carried on as if nothing had happened. We indeed knew this piece and this passage of music inside and out. We had been drilled on this passage over and over, just in case anything should happen in performance. Reflecting on this gaffe, I felt sorry for the other conductors of these youth choirs. The concert was a success, and Elmer made our inaugural YCIC event an historic moment. I learned from this experience to be as prepared as you can, but to be aware of unforeseen moments.

In 2001, I worked for the Elmer Iseler Singers as their development manager for a year. Elmer (when he was alive) was always very gracious to me and was interested in meeting and building relationships with other TMYC alumni. I was closely exposed to the choral flame burning inside of him. He passed his torch of passion for choral music to me and others. Elmer was cognizant of his influence and responsibility as a Canadian choral pioneer. My involvement with TMYC opened many doors for me, with professional contacts in both business and the arts.

One of the important things that we did as youth singers during the Christmas seasons of the 1980s and 1990s was to assemble and wassail around the prestigious area of Rosedale in Toronto. Our yearly host was Laura Schatz, a Toronto soprano soloist, educator, and now artistic director of many G&S productions. Initially this Christmas event was intended as an Ontario Youth Choir (OYC) party and for alumni of the choir.

Over the years, Laura expanded the party and invited her other singing friends. Laura would invite me to be a part of these wonderful holiday parties. After we had toured many homes within Toronto's established Rosedale set with our harmonious caroling, we would come back to her home, have some traditional mulled wine, and sing Handel's *Messiah* choral selections from beginning to end. These holiday events were wonderful and so much fun!

Before we would leave for our caroling tour route, we'd sing for Laura's grandfather, the former Governor General of Canada, Roland Michener. Always gracious, he was very enthusiastic about our music. Mr. Michener was a tremendous supporter and patron to choral music in Canada. I've included the picture below to bookmark this memory of Maureen Forrester and The Right Honorable Roland Michener.

Maureen Forrester and the late Governor General, Roland Michener
(Goldschmidt Collection)

From the fall of 2007 until May of 2010, I served as Director of Marketing and Communications for the Orpheus Choir of Toronto. Combined with Chorus Niagara, London Pro Musica, and Orchestra London Canada, we had the opportunity to perform the Canadian premiere (and subsequent three city tour) of Sir Paul McCartney's second choral work, "Ecce Cor Meum." Encompassing the southern and southwestern regions of Ontario, our concert and tour were picked up by the AP Canadian wire services, resulting in national as well as international coverage of this choral event.

Sir Paul wrote to Robert Cooper, conductor and producer of this tour, that he was deeply touched by our wanting to perform his work. He said:

119

"It's always a pleasant surprise to think that someone would complement me and my music in this way. I wish you the greatest of evenings, and although I will not be able to get there in person, I certainly will be there in spirit." Sir Paul provided flowers for each of the three performance venues during the tour. Bringing together 250 singers on stage with an orchestra, this experience was another highlight in my choral career!

Through my association with Robert Cooper and the Orpheus Choir of Toronto, I have had the privilege of working with the well-established choral scene and international guest artists in Toronto. I had the wonderful pleasure to meet and build relationships with choral legends such as Sir David Willcocks and John Rutter.

Meeting Sir David Willcocks with Elaine in 2001 (ECG Photo Collection)

In November of 2008, the combined mass chorus of Orpheus Choir of Toronto and Chorus Niagara had the privilege of working with Sir David's and his son, Jonathan Willcocks', composition, "Lux Perpetua." Sir David conducted this piece with the mass chorus in St. Catharines and Toronto.

Sir David Willcocks, at the age of ninety-four, passed away in September 2015. He was a wonderful friend and colleague to me. Not only was he a "choral icon," but he was extremely generous to any young singer, musician, or choral conductor just beginning in their careers. I so enjoyed our chats via email once we initially became friends in 2001, and we corresponded until 2010. Throughout our emails (he insisted that I call him "David"), I shared with him my passion for the Royal Family, especially with the choral anthems performed during royal events.

In 2002, the Queen celebrated her Golden Jubilee, and Sir David was honoured to be asked to conduct a mass choir performing at the base of Buckingham Palace. He conducted Handel's "Coronation Anthems," Perry's "I Was Glad," Elgar's "Land of Hope and Glory," and Britain's national anthem, "God Save the Queen" ... plus a few new compositions from some inaugural composers selected to participate in this event, combined with folk songs from across many Commonwealth nations.

Within a few weeks of the Royal celebration, a package from David arrived in my mailbox. He'd sent me a copy of the Jubilee weekend program with a personal note in the package about these new composers and the full program of music that was performed throughout the day. The Queen and the Duke of Edinburgh journeyed in the Golden State Coach from Buckingham Palace (where the choral music would begin) to St. Paul's Cathedral for the Jubilee's significant program.

I was totally blown away that David would think of me, and I sent him an email right away to thank him for his generosity. I had taped that "live event" and later went back to watch the Jubilee program, following along with David's outstanding choral programming for that "once in a lifetime event!"

Sir David Willcock's choral legacy will never be forgotten. He touched so many lives internationally with his passion for this art form, and he was a true mentor to many. If you'd like to know more about Sir David's legacy, I'd encourage you to purchase the book *A Life in Music: Conversations with Sir David Willcocks and Friends* (Owen, 2008).

In November 2004, we were given the opportunity to perform with John Rutter for the Canadian premiere of "Mass of the Children" and "Feel the Spirit." The Toronto performance was a real celebration for us, having John Rutter as our guest conductor for the fortieth anniversary celebration of the Orpheus Choir of Toronto.

While involved with Robert Cooper, along with some additional male voices from the Orpheus Choir of Toronto, I was asked to sing with Chorus Niagara. In July 2010, we performed at Hamilton's Copps Coliseum with two performances as the in-house chorus for *Star Wars* in Concert. After a few weeks of rehearsal, we sang fifteen to twenty minutes' worth of choral music. What a wonderful treat to sing with a sixty-piece orchestra as well as have the opportunity to connect and meet with Anthony Daniels, "C-3PO" himself. Mr. Daniels was very animated, revving us up to get into "character" of the Sanskrit lyrics, which required much diction and character. Anthony was also very generous in providing a chorus member's photo opportunity. Mr. Daniels was the narrator of this amazing concert, complete with film excerpts from the entire *Star Wars* series, set to the incredible music of John Williams.

PRIMING MY VOCAL SKILLS FOR UNIVERSITY

Being with other young people and adults who shared my passion for choral singing was so important to me during my teenage to university years. One time during this period, our group of TMYC singers sang in Toronto's underground subway, which had similar acoustics to the tubes in London, U.K. We did this Bach selection and experienced the magnificent acoustics of choral sound in the platform area. We were bold! We were vibrant! We all sang, stirring our spirits to sing … with future dreams of potential careers in vocal and the choral arts. Considering my ADHD issues, TMYC helped me focus on my weekly musical and rehearsal activities. I learned many valuable time management skills.

After working full-time at The Children's Bookstore, I needed to get my voice and piano skills primed. In preparing for university admissions, I would work on my RCM Grade Five piano examination and its theory requirements. These two lessons would add more expense to my budget. Most music students that I knew survived from paycheque to paycheque. When I did get into a university music program, I regretted not being properly trained in music theory. Now I had to catch up, and I did my best by reviewing old tests and examination papers.

Debbie Rutledge (related to my best friend, Michael) was an excellent piano teacher. She understood my learning limitations and my difficulty with the breakdown of numbers—the math part of music. When a rhythmic problem would occur, Debbie knew how to break down the rhythms so that it would compute in my brain. We got on very well. I passed my RCM Grade Five piano exam with first class honours.

One of the wonderful things about living with church friends in the Beaches of Toronto was that they owned a beautiful mahogany Steinway baby grand piano, situated in a dining room, finished all in wood. No one in the family played often. It was like practicing in a studio every day, as this room and the piano were at my disposal. How glorious! The acoustics from this room were truly first class!

Finally, I was ready to do my admission juries for three university applications. The time came for me to audition. My first audition was for the Faculty of Music, University of Toronto. My three contrasting vocal pieces went well in performance. One of my adjudicators was one of the toughest critics within the University of Toronto Music Faculty. Canadian composer and old-school British choirmaster, Dr. Derek Holman, would be appraising my vocal performance!

Dr. Holman seemed pleased with my voice and performance. Then came the ear training and sight reading. The sight singing part went well, but the ear training element was a disaster! I made a mistake and gave the wrong answer to a musical interval question. Dr. Holman roared at me like a lion! Needless to say, I didn't want to go to U of T after that negative experience. Academically, there was no way, due to my ADHD, that I would be able to handle their program.

In 2001, Robert Cooper asked me to come back and work with him again as TMYC choir manager. The Toronto Children's Chorus and Opera in Concert Chorus, combined with TMYC, had been asked to come together as one choral ensemble to give Dr. Holman a wonderful birthday party gift. On May 15, 2001, the choral community of Toronto celebrated the seventieth birthday celebration of Dr. Holman in a gala concert event entitled "A Little Birthday Tribute Concert." Robert conducted the ensemble, which performed many of Holman's well-known choral compositions. It was a grand occasion!

During the reception following the concert, I had the opportunity to speak with Dr. Holman and asked him if he remembered taking a large strip off a very young baritone singer in 1982. He knew he could be a harsh taskmaster at times. With a twinkle in his eye, he responded: "Are you sure that was me who treated you so badly?" The conversation continued as he asked me which university I chose. When I told him that I indeed attended the University of Western Ontario, he responded to me that I had made a "very good choice."

MY YEARS AT WESTERN'S FACULTY OF MUSIC

I was accepted to the University of Western Ontario in 1982. I practically lived at the Faculty of Music (FOM). During the first two years as a "music major," the workload alone is compared to one's first or second year in the School of Medicine. Music students put in the same amount of study and practical experience.

My time was spent with private lessons, practice/rehearsal sessions, sight singing, and ear training courses. The constant workload, especially in music history and theory courses, caused me much grief. I lacked grounding in the art of academic essay writing. It wouldn't be until the late 1990s that I'd get a much better handle on my ADHD issues. The use of computerized equipment and voice activated software (within a university setting) would be a great asset for me. In the early 1980s, my essay writing skills were very poor. Unaware, I left out words in my papers and had problems with syntax from paragraph to paragraph. Once this problem was pointed out to me, I corrected my errors, and slowly my marks greatly improved!

The Faculty of Music (FOM) was a beautiful place to be during the early 1980s, as everyone got to know everyone's name. Our first-year class had 150 full-time registered students. As a mature student, I decided that I would join the Music Student Council to get to know other students. Unafraid to meet people, I met many students from first-year to graduate music students. Some of these friends would later become a vital network of Canadian vocal and choral music contacts. Many have remained good friends to today.

Just before each Christmas exam period, there would be a huge Christmas tree in the centre of the student lounge, and it would be decorated to perfection! All the music students and faculty would gather around, and we'd sing some carols or popular songs celebrating the season. It was a wonderful moment of solidarity.

For my ensemble music credit, I set my goal to be accepted into the Faculty of Music Singers (FOM Singers) in the first year of my degree program. The ensemble was directed by the late Professor Deral Johnson (DJ). Professor Johnson's reputation as a choral conductor and educator was legendary. I wanted to learn and apprentice under this great yet humble man. Dr. Deral Johnson, known to all as "DJ," mentored many students during his thirty-year career.

My audition went well for Professor Johnson and, once he learned that I had sung under Robert Cooper and was an alumnus of the TMYC, he welcomed me into his choir. For many years the FOM Singers were the cream of the crop and highly regarded for one's accredited choral ensemble.

Musicians with other instrumental majors but who could sing were welcomed to audition. I was so excited about being welcomed into this elite choral group in my first year in university. It meant I had to work very hard with my ongoing repertoire. Despite my learning disability, my sight-reading skills have never been a problem. Just give me a challenging piece of choral music to sing and I could do it! If it was a difficult piece, I liked the opportunity to "dig in" and do one's best, and for that moment my personal self-esteem was at its peak! At various times throughout the rehearsal, DJ would come and stand in front of an individual and would sing off key or make funny sounds to throw them off. It must have been my British-Scottish temperament, but I was determined that I wouldn't be influenced by his interference.

DJ's philosophical approach stressed: "You are an individual singer, and you are an integral part as a member of any choral ensemble. At times, you may have the opportunity to be a solo singer and will need to be secure and strong; however, you must also blend within your ensemble. Other times, you will need to sing out and hear your own part within an established quartet." From this approach, we would sing in quartets for most of our rehearsals and concerts. I love singing in SATB quartets. If you don't know your music, you're sunk!

Being involved in FOM "Singers" also meant that we would do a lot of travelling on the weekends, as well as concerts during our school term. The repertoire would include music from the Renaissance, the Baroque, the Classical, and the Romantic eras and all the way to modern music. Our goal was to leave the audiences wanting more. When DJ would acknowledge the applause of the audience, the characteristic flick of his raised hand meant that it was time for "his Singers" to take our well-deserved bows.

Mrs. Marie Johnson was our very fine accompanist and organist. We would sing in Latin, French, German, English, and Russian. In 1983–84, we the "Singers'" were eligible for a Canada Council Cultural Exchange grant with the University of British Columbia (UBC) Faculty Singers. The grant covered all expenses. The tour would stop in various locations around B.C and Victoria for then days in February. Along with the tour, we would be involved with a few choral workshops.

The weather in London, Ontario, was simply awful the day of departure, with blizzard snow conditions. It was my first time flying over the Rockies, and the sun was just setting over the mountains. It was a sight to see! We arrived in Vancouver on a February spring-like day that was simply glorious!

Due to it being close to "reading week" for Western students, and knowing that we would be missing some classes while on tour, the singers experienced extra stress. Therefore, some singers got ill during the middle part of the tour. I learned how to preserve my voice.

One of my personal memories from the tour was singing in St. Andrews United Church on a warm, spring-like Sunday morning. We assembled to sing at the altar of the church as part of the service. There stood the most amazing arrangement of daffodils that I had ever seen! Being an April baby, daffodils are my favourite flower. Just as we were in the middle of our choral piece ("Lux Altera" by E. Fissinger), an amazing burst of light came through the top of the stained-glass window and then radiated on this flower arrangement. From that day until the present, I have been crazy about daffodils in April. I couldn't focus on Professor Johnson's conducting and on the text of the music that we were singing; God was getting my attention! I could hardly sing the words from this Latin text, which translated meant: "Let light eternal shine on them, O Lord, with thy saints forever, for thou art merciful. Rest eternal, grant them, O Lord, and let perpetual light shine on them."

Looking back now, I see this divine visitation as the beginning of the Holy Spirit speaking to me through text and music. I had clearly witnessed His presence and His power! He was speaking to me, probing me to come deeper into the stirring of my soul!

CHAPTER ELEVEN
MOVING UP AND ONWARDS WITH MY MANAGEMENT SKILLS

Old songs or phrases from the 1930–40s stick with me. Looking back on this period of my life feels reminiscent of an old Cole Porter song, "What a Swell Party It Is," or, in my case, was. This party period in my career was the beginning of many firsts in reaching out and trying new things. Some of the ideas or projects that I created in my apprenticeship years greatly succeeded—and others failed. These growing years eventually led me into a passion for arts administration, marketing, development, and fundraising.

I married Gwen Woods in July 1984. Once back from our honeymoon in September, Gwen and I began to settle into working and living in London, Ontario. This city would become my home for the next thirteen years. Placed on academic probation due to my deficiencies by Western (University) required some time off. For me, that meant one complete year away from my music studies.

I applied to several arts administration positions in the city, but at that time I didn't have any previous full-time work experience. Then I applied for and received a full-time position at Sam the Record Man as the Classical Music Sales Associate. Working in this store was the beginning of a different kind of education for me—seeing how the other half lived and survived. Our weekly paycheques meant that Sam employees learned to live on very little money.

The franchise owner of the store was Phil, a well-respected businessman and restaurant entrepreneur. Phil was a family man who also dabbled in the entertainment field. Through Ticketron, he sold many tickets to rock and roll concerts all over North America. Phil was always very respectful of me and my Classical music background.

He shielded me from seeing employees who enjoyed smoking a joint or two in the back of the store, or from watching these employees take drugs at the end of the workday. I soon learned that employees who were once former roadies, booking agents, or performers were still waiting for "their big break" well into their thirties. The drug culture and the heavy metal music that they liked to play at the end of the work day were more than I could stand. After eight months, I decided that I would soon resign my position and look for something more in my field.

One of the perks of working for Phil at the London franchise of Sam the Record Man was the opportunity to have first crack at purchasing tickets through the Ticketron computer right there in the store. As a staff member, I could purchase good tickets to The Jackson Five Victory Tour starring Michael Jackson at Toronto's CNE Stadium. Our seats were about ten rows from the stage. It was an amazing concert, as Michael performed his trademark song "Billie Jean" and danced the moonwalk. The Jackson Five also performed many of their seasoned hits. How very sad that Michael's name and career would be so tarnished.

One of my former colleagues, Lisa Brandt, and I worked together in the record store. She is now a well-known Canadian Toronto Broadcaster and MC. Lisa was trying to establish her broadcasting career with the local CKSL Radio Station. As a DJ, she worked many late-night shifts; however, she couldn't get a full-time contract at the station. Whenever they had an open spot, Lisa was there, willing to gain more experience and on-air exposure. I enjoyed working with Lisa. She would make me laugh or she'd fill me in on all the staff news. We'd talk about all the arising new artists and band gossip in the city. Lisa also agreed with Phil that this wasn't the right place for me. I just didn't fit in.

In April of 1985, it was time for Phil to evaluate my job performance. He recognized my challenging work and the way that I had made the Classical music department a place of expertise. There had been a slight increase of sales in my section since I'd been hired to manage it, but Phil was laying me off. With many contacts in the city, he made a few calls on my behalf in search of another job. Phil set up a meeting for me to connect with either the communications or marketing departments with Orchestra London Canada (OLC).

In the spring of 1985, my apprenticeship years in arts administration began with OLC. Depending on how the government grants were flowing from year to year, I had either full-time or part-time status. As an apprentice, I could continue to learn valuable skills in arts administration, stage management, public relations, marketing, and fundraising. I worked in this milieu environment for four years until the spring of 1989. I also gained valuable work experience at the Orchestra's telemarketing subscription campaigns for two years and then worked at the box office. I was promoted to work as Marketing Assistant to the Director of Marketing.

Once I learned the ropes of how OLC was operated and managed, I learned how I could be a good administrator and promoter. This position was the beginning of my learning how to think outside of the box. I worked as a contracted person. The full-time staff recognized my passion and natural skills. My input on future marketing ideas was especially welcomed during our promotions campaigns. Certain individuals in the office would proofread my work before anything went out to the public or the media. There would be times when I would leave out words in the copy, and either my spelling or syntax was not correct in my written work. This would require someone in my department to "edit my work" before it would be published. This agreement within my department was my way of compensating for my writing disability.

LEARNING HOW TO CULTIVATE MAJOR DONORS AND WORK WITH A DIFFICULT BOSS

In 1985 when I worked for OLC, I met many hard-working staff and board and committee members dedicated to the orchestra's community profile. I had many opportunities to meet and cultivate sponsors and major gift donors, many of whom were recognized as members of the Who's Who of London.

At first, I didn't know how to conduct myself when dealing with these high-profile individuals. I was, however, an apprentice, and I was teachable. When I was told to do something important, I did it! Wanting to become an excellent arts administrator, I listened, learned, and watched, asking lots of questions. Truthfully, I was as green as grass when it came to presenting one's image to a potential sponsor or donor; however, I wanted any donor to recognize my zeal and passion for the arts.

One of these wealthy individuals that greatly blessed me with her wisdom and her time was the late Martha Blackburn. Martha Blackburn was then CEO of the Blackburn Group that had business interests all over Canada, and holdings in all the major media outlets (in television, print, and radio) for the southwest regions of Ontario. Her father had begun the mighty Blackburn Media Group empire, and she had the money and heart to invest in many arts related projects.

Martha was very committed to the growth and the well-being of Orchestra London. Martha had a passion for horses and especially for the art of dressage, and she had barns and a stadium on her estate to accommodate her interests. Martha offered her estate for an Orchestra fundraiser, and I helped coordinate the event. Becoming interested in my career, Martha taught me many vital steps in the ways to build trust with a future donor.

I learned so much from Martha and watching her function in a crowd. She taught and coached me on these initial steps and then let me go "solo" to try out these skills for myself. Martha then informed me that I was a natural in this business and gave me some pointers. Martha's coaching certainly boosted my level of self-confidence.

I was warned that due to her financial status within the community, Martha could insist upon her own way. On the contrary, however, I never found her to be difficult with me. Sadly, Martha passed away in her early forties from a heart attack. At that sad moment, London lost one of its greatest arts patrons.

In 1987, OLC wanted to find out if I could qualify for a Canada Council grant that would provide me with more senior level administration experience working exclusively with the Executive Director of the Orchestra. This required filling out a grant application outlining the objectives of the arts organization. Granted an interview, I caught a flight to Ottawa for the day to the Canada Council's national headquarters, at their expense. Soon I was grilled by many council members. It would seem to me that I was entrée of the day! Until I entered the board room, I didn't know that I was being interviewed by a panel of at least ten people. Help! This scenario was very stressful, and I felt my blood pressure soar.

One of the panelists started firing questions at me about various aspects of the grant-funded position and the duties that I would be undertaking. Was I aware that the funds, if given, would be used specifically here and there? How would I best make use of these resources? It was like they were speaking Russian. I had not been properly coached!

The Executive Director (ED) thought this grant would be an easy sell—almost guaranteed to obtain the funds. I was told that this interview would be low-key, a formality, in order that I could be approved and then hired full-time by the Orchestra. The Orchestra needed this grant for them to continue my employment on either a part-time or a full-time basis. It was my first experience with the politics. Obviously, I needed to learn how to play the game.

The Canada Council grant application was denied to me. Enduring this magnitude of an emotional interview like this, I have never forgotten this experience! Believe me, if I'm ever in that type of situation again, I will certainly plumb the depths of preparation.

To get to know the inner workings of the Orchestra, I sought out and made friends with Alexis Hauser, then artistic director and conductor of the Orchestra. He was an outstanding musician for the city and our organization. During his tenure with OLC, the Faculty of Music and London Pro Musica had the opportunity to learn more about the amazing symphonic or choral works, such as Beethoven's Ninth Symphony and Mahler's Eighth Symphony (Symphony of a Thousand). Under this European-trained and internationally known maestro, we would all work together, hearing Hauser's interpretation of these magnificent works.

When Alexis was in his office, I would go in and have personal chats with him. We'd discuss the details of preceding concerts and the repertoire that he had chosen, or chat about the general OLC concert series. I learned so much from watching Alexis as he worked with the musicians and the board of administration. When he greeted the public, he was always so positive. As I later observed, every conductor brands their image and personae into the community.

In 1983, the Faculty of Music at the University of Western Ontario hosted an International Gustav Mahler Symposium in combination with the opening of The Mahler-Rosé Collection in the Music library. The Music Faculty's website posted:

> This Collection represents a significant addition to the knowledge of Gustav Mahler and will be required material for any serious scholar involved in research into the life and times of the composer and, for that matter, the life and times of his brother-in-law, Arnold Rosé, or his nephew, Alfred Rosé.[3]

There are over six hundred personal letters and private documents that belonged to Arnold Rosé (brother-in-law to Mahler) and Alfred Rosé, the nephew of the great maestro. Professor Alfred Rosé held these personal belongings when his family emigrated from war-torn Germany to Britain and then to Canada in the 1940s. These important letters and other artifacts were given to the University of Western Ontario's Faculty of Music by Maria Rosé, the widow of Professor Rosé. There was also personal correspondence with Professor Rosé from the estate of Dr. Nicholas Goldschmidt, who would become my dear friend and mentor.

---

[3] "The Gustav Mahler Alfred Rosé Collection," *Western Libraries*, https://www.lib.uwo.ca/music/gmar.html. (accessed April 2, 2018).

In celebration of this amazing collection given to the Faculty of Music, the symposium ended with Maestro Hauser and the efforts of Orchestra London Canada, London Pro Musica, UWO's choral division, and the Faculty of Music Singers performing this rarely performed and very expensive Mahler's 8th Symphony, known as The Symphony of a Thousand. That was another once in a lifetime musical experience for me—working with OLC and singing this rarely performed choral work.

In the fall season of 1988–1989, I was asked if I would like to volunteer and gain further arts management experience with London Pro Musica (LPM). LPM was the community choir of sixty voices in which I sang. I would be their publicity director for the upcoming season. The Verdi Requiem was the last concert in the season, and we combined with the Kitchener-Waterloo Philharmonic Choir under the direction of then Howard Dyck, artistic director of both choirs. Our Verdi Requiem concert ticket price in London was $25 per ticket—unheard of in today's prices.

During this time, I was working part-time at the Orchestra and part-time at Canada's then national department store, Eaton's. In the late 1980s, the Orchestra couldn't afford to hire me full-time, so I worked on a contract basis to gain the experience on a two-city concert tour. Once it was announced that Maureen Forrester would be one of our guest artists on the roster of our Verdi Requiem, I was desperate for the experience. I accepted this challenge with LPM and began to represent both the OLC's and the LPM's marketing needs.

At the beginning of LPM's season, I told my boss, the ED of OLC, of this once in a lifetime opportunity to be able to work with Maureen Forrester. I wondered if it would be all right with him if I gained further experience working for both arts organizations in the same season. He assured me that he didn't have a problem, as long as my volunteer work didn't interfere with my administrative duties at OLC. My title was Assistant to the Marketing Director. I wanted to document our conversation and get his signature on a memo, indicating that he approved of this venture; however, I didn't follow up on this idea or create the document. Had I done so, I would have had a signed document to use in my legal defense for a miscommunication issue.

As the 1988–89 season ended, LPM was getting more publicity throughout the city of London and Southwestern Ontario. Due to our involvement with the Verdi Requiem and its international cast of featured soloists, we (the marketing committee of the choir) were using many media PSAs (Public Service Announcements) ads. For the first time in the driver's seat, I was learning how to write for both radio and television. As a result, I was given my first opportunity to work with a CFPL TV's senior producer from concept stage to finished product on a PSA for television with his advertising crew. I found this experience very rewarding—my very first TV promo commercial! Of course, I still have a copy of this video commercial in my media collection.

We had created radio and television PSAs, combined with some print ads, with very little advertising dollars. I administered and supervised all this PR and marketing activity. We even tried a new promotional aid publicizing our concerts with hand bills. The handbills were stapled to all outgoing dry cleaning from the local dry cleaner who, by the way, became a new sponsor of the choir a bit later. The ED at OLC was furious that I was working part-time with OLC and that the other event was getting more publicity and creative energy than any upcoming concerts at Orchestra London Canada's current season.

Two weeks before the Verdi Requiem concert was about to take place, I got an afternoon phone call at home from the ED, telling me that he was very disappointed in me because all of my creative ideas were going toward LPM's needs and not to the Orchestra. Informing me that he had received a handbill from the dry cleaners, the ED was ballistic in his temper and tone to me over the phone. He asked why I wasn't using similar ideas for the OLC. I reminded him of our earlier conversation and his permission for me to work with LPM. He tried to deny that he had given me permission to do so. Lesson learned: That was the first and the last time that I let myself be involved in any business dealings without having a contract created or a letter of agreement to protect myself.

Toward the end of our phone conversation, I reminded him that I was only working at the office part-time. And then he fired me—right there and over the phone. He told me to come into the office and pick up my personal belongings. Some of the seasoned employees had seen many executive directors of the Orchestra come and go. I found out later that by firing me, this individual had lost a lot of respect from the seasoned staff. They were very upset that he had tried to use me in his schemes of involving the Canada Council grant, and now this experience.

Because I worked for the Orchestra for over four years, I had friends in the office who respected my work and my marketing talents. They felt that the ED's method of firing me was further evidence that this person did not know how to conduct himself as a professional. As a business leader, the ED's job was to work with many donors and sponsors who represented the political views in London community. Within two years of my dismissal from OLC in 1989, this ED disgraced himself by some very unprofessional behaviour by twisting the truth to the Board of Directors. His contract was not renewed.

I was physically and emotionally devastated by being fired from OLC. I loved working there, and the staff were amazing! I wanted the opportunity to learn from both arts organizations, especially in putting together and administering a two-city tour. That was very exciting for me, and working for both arts groups consumed my thoughts. What shook me to the core was that I was very naïve; there was no guile or subterfuge on my part to do my best only for OLC. To be accused of not doing my best and putting my volunteer position over my paid position was not true. For many months after my firing I would re-live this scenario and wonder if there was anything that I could have done to prevent leaving OLC.

After all this activity and energy in making the Verdi Requiem promotion a considerable success, I received all sorts of city-wide compliments. Many wondered, "Who was this person behind all of this promotional and media activity that had generated such a buzz in such a brief time?" Some of the best compliments concerning the team's public relations and marketing efforts came from long-time choir members of LPM who informed me that they had never seen or heard so much publicity, and that many movers and shakers in the city were beginning to take notice of our choir. Knowing that I had finished the job with style was very rewarding. Yahoo!

But I didn't have a job to come back to after the choral concerts. At that time, my mother invited me to take a trip to Florida and share the load and responsibility of bringing my grandmother home. I was in much need of a period of down-time. I welcomed the opportunity to refocus.

In the fall of 2014, I received the sad news that OLC was no more. Due to severe financial difficulties, the arts organization went bankrupt. I was very sad for the musicians, artists, and arts administrative personnel who had been the backbone of this organization and community for over fifty years. Looking back, I'm not sure I would have made such personal and professional progress working for a larger arts organization. I do hope that OLC can regroup and make a comeback as a strong community orchestra.

In the summer of 1990, we received the news that Gwen was expecting our first child. To prepare, we would need a financial plan. In other words, I needed a job. After my brief holiday with my family in Florida, I accepted a temporary position as a collections officer for a collections agency. After all, I had numerous telemarketing experience with arts campaigns. This job primarily dealt with student loans, and I hated it! I could make the payment arrangements with the clients that I was dealing with over the phone; however, the tactics that the other collection officers used, and the games that they played to get their clients to pay the bills, were not for me!

Christina was born in the spring of 1991. I stayed in the collection agency job for about six months until I was offered a position as corporate bookings manager for Second City Comedy Club and Restaurant, formerly of London, Ontario.

Now this job I loved! With my connections to the London Chamber of Commerce and the Ad and Sales Club, I was promoting potential bookings for corporate contracts, and I ended up booking many clients. Some of these interested patrons wanted to use this venue for fundraising ventures or incentives for their staff who had worked on arduous work assignments. The contacts that I made are now some of Canada's greatest comedians and performers. They all began from their initial roots in comedy and are now alumni from this short lived Second City, London, Ontario troupe.

One of those cast members from that assembled Second City London alumni is Linda Kash, daughter of my dear mentor, Maureen Forrester. Linda is an accomplished actress, having appeared in many starring roles herself or opposite some of Hollywood's current roster of A talent. As Linda ages gracefully, I see so much of her mother's looks and bubbly personality on screen. I met Linda for the first time at a Canadian Opera Company event and told her of our joint connection. Even though I was on the management staff, she warmly welcomed me as alumni from the Second City London organization.

The dreaded GST (Goods and Sales Tax) was then just being imposed on Canadians coast to coast in 1991 and early into 1992. Second City London had many American visitors that would trek the two plus hours to come across the border to London to take advantage of our Canadian dollar and spend tourist dollars in the city by participating in one of these amazing, yet truly Canadian, comedy shows. Canadians, especially Londoners, were then concerned about spending too much money on their entertainment with this newly added tax forced upon them. The famed Canadian comedy entrepreneur Andrew Alexander owned this company, and his sister and brother-in-law managed the London, Ontario operation. They jointly decided that, due to the GST, business had begun to dry up. As a result, they would move their operations to Detroit, MI, which meant that I was out of a job—yet again!

I'd had enough of this on again/off again working relationship in the arts! Just about six months earlier, I decided to create my own arts management agency. I began to make connections with some of the summer festivals contacts and developed and marketed my public relations and fundraising services to individual artists and their agents. I had heard that London was about to establish its own International Children's Festival through chairperson Glenda Pennington (former arts consultant for the Board of Education for the City of London). I wanted to be on this general advisory committee and learn how an international arts festival is created and maintained.

Being on this advisory committee was an amazing learning experience! I am so proud to be associated with the London International Children's

Festival, which was in operation for twenty plus years. As a learning experience for me, I chose to volunteer my services and watch and learn. As part of the festival marketing committee, I worked and networked with some of the best minds in marketing and arts administration, combined with others who represented business and the arts contacts for many national and international businesses within the city. By being on this general committee, I made contacts with graphic designers, administrators, consultants, producers, and educators from both the Catholic and public schools of London. I still have the proposal of the initial festival. It's a very detailed document that I still refer to when I'm working with a client who wants to begin and develop a two or three year action plan for creating an international festival.

As I was a new dad during the official opening of the Children's Festival, I will always associate my early years with Christina as a newborn in the spring of 1991 with the Grand Opening events. During the opening festivities of the event in June, we took her to the festival in her stroller. Somewhere I have a picture of Christina holding onto an original balloon of the festival, in her stroller, with her dad by her side, looking on proudly.

During my second year with the festival, I co-produced an outdoor children's concert featuring Linda Bovey, a hearing-impaired children's artist who had appeared many times on *Sesame Street* and was a character actress in the movie *Children of a Lesser God*. I helped program the children's choir that would precede our guest artist. That was another rewarding experience! I was so sad to learn that in 2014, the London International Children's Festival was no more. Another local and international cultural festival gone—just like the dinosaur age!

As I began to make many contacts in the entertainment industry, I felt that God was calling me home to Hamilton. I can't describe this feeling except to say that something deep within my heart and soul was at peace with the thought of being home in Hamilton. The lustre of living and working in London had already begun to lose it shimmer. For thirteen years I had lived in this community, worshipped in several churches, and created a name for myself as both a Christian soloist and arts administrator. I had worked hard in all my arts experiences, gaining valuable on-the-job training. I knew, however, that in London I had learned all that I could, and I had accomplished all I could professionally.

There would be more opportunities for me and my family working and living in the greater Toronto area (known as the GTA). Many new entertainment options lay just around the corner for me. At the same time, I had also learned how to hear the Lord's voice directing my career options and opening new job opportunities. This voice—God's voice—grew louder and louder inside of my heart. It was time to come home! Indeed, God had work for me to do in Hamilton. I had such peace about the future and the beginning moments of developing my Christian broadcasting television career and ministry.

"There is a Way"

Written for the Baptist "Focus" Group as its theme song in 1986
Words and Music by W. Ian Walker

CHORUS

There, there is a way;
Open your eyes and follow His way.
Let the Spirit transform your life,
Change your strife,
Into powerful meaning and praise.

1ST VERSE

Some days can be weary and long;
You can't cope with one more problem today.
You long to be alone, yet there's nowhere to meditate and pray.
Then Jesus cries out "Why walk alone? Ease your burden on me.
You're a child of mine!"
Leave your cares of the world and its sin, oh so far behind.

CHORUS

2ND VERSE

There's a feeling of peace that I found as Jesus took hold of my life,
And when days of despair are near, I lean on Him.
He gives me the faith to trust His Word;
I no longer doubt the power He has,
What a marvellous change He has made in my life.

CHORUS

CHAPTER TWELVE
THE STIRRING WITHIN, GROWING DEEPER WITH GOD

Broadsided! In 1989, I was involved in a car accident. Had a passenger been sitting in the right side of my car, he or she would not have survived. The combination of the impact of the oncoming car and the momentum of my vehicle sent me airborne across two lanes of traffic. Thank the Lord there was no passenger in the right seat of my car! I sustained some severe bruising and a whiplash. A year later, I could return to work. Unbearable pain in my neck and lower back required daily chiropractic treatments for at least six weeks. Looking back, 1989 was a year of deep soul searching as I asked God, "What are your plans for my life?"

Around 2:00 one morning, I was in a lot of pain in both my neck and lower back. Unable to rest, much less sleep, I turned on the Crossroads' program *Nite Lite*. The topic was having a personal relationship with the Holy Spirit. I understood what having a relationship with Jesus was about; however, I had never heard of having a relationship with the Holy Spirit.

Turning full face to the TV audience, the host invited people to ask the Holy Spirit into their lives and to fill up the voids in their relationship with God that years of "religion" had tried in vain to fill. I was curious. I was in pain. I thought, *What have I to lose?* So I prayed the suggested prayer. Afterwards, I felt that it was time to rest. I wasn't on any pain medication except a regular regimen of Tylenol as directed by my doctor.

I climbed into bed. Immediately, an open vision appeared before me and I saw a graphic wheel of fire of multiple colours, like a disco ball on fire. I watched it revolve around my entire bedroom. I tried to wake up Gwen so that she could participate in this supernatural experience. She was, however, sleeping so soundly I couldn't wake her up. Deciding that I needed some time to process what I had or had not seen, I didn't tell her about this open vision until a few days later.

During this open vision, a burst of fire shot out from the multi-coloured fire ball and hit me on the top of my head. At that moment, a healing began. Immediately following this supernatural visitation, I had greater mobility in my neck and lower back without any further pain. With a few additional touches from God, the pain was eventually gone from my body. Praise God! This heavenly encounter was my second supernatural experience in the presence of God. At the age of seventeen, I heard His audible voice speaking and calling my name, and now this experience!

As a result of the wheel of fire vision in my bedroom, my passion for God and His presence and His purpose in my life was rekindled to full flame. This open vision not only restored my health, but my faith. As it was in my youth, I began to clearly hear the voice of the Spirit of God leading and directing me in the ways that I should go. I was moving into a deeper faith level. Through visions and dreams at night, God was directing me to follow His plan. Delightfully, it was the beginning of exploring a future career move in Christian music broadcasting and video production.

During that same supernatural event, I also experienced the presence of the enemy and his cohorts. I sensed a spirit of fear coming at me from the other side of the bed. This evil spirit tried to come all over me and literally tried to cover my mouth and block my voice. This presence of darkness was icy cold. Relief came when I spoke the name of Jesus!

The demonic spirit instantly fled. After this open vision, my passion for God and reading His Word was restored. Also, I read many Christian biographies concerning brokenness and healing. I became a living sponge.

At the time of the accident, I was driving a 1984 White Toyota Tercel, which I called my white Trojan horse. After the accident, the car was fully restored to its former glory. In the fall of 1989, I was involved in three potential accidents with this car. My London chiropractor said, "There must be something about this car that attracts people to meet up with you, but I don't want to be near you on the road." These accidents were not my fault and there was definitely a sense of "spiritual warfare" going on. I would cry out to God and ask that His angels come immediately around me. I remember just calling out, "Jesus, help me!" When each of these potential accidents occurred, I got out of the car to investigate the damage. There was none! However, the car following too closely behind me had severe damage.

In April of 1990 I celebrated my thirtieth birthday. I sensed a stirring in my soul that God was about to do something spectacular. I was spending time in the Word and asking God to clarify things that I needed to understand. I wanted to receive the Holy Ghost impartation of speaking in tongues. I was hungry for God's Spirit. Three days before my birthday, while at a church event, I received this impartation. Immediately I thought, *Isn't this just like God to give me this gift, just as Jesus received his impartation at the beginning of his thirtieth year?*

I had always taken a keen interest in Christian Contemporary Music (CCM). During my prayer times with the Lord, He began to download many visions and dreams of me being involved with CCM and its industry. I sought God to provide a contact in broadcasting. I needed someone to assist me to fulfill this personal vision. I knew nothing of this medium or how to do anything in Christian television. I just had Jesus as my executive producer.

I discovered an amazing quote from Oswald Chambers, author of the best-selling devotional, *My Utmost for His Highest*. Chambers speaks about visions from God and how they are to process and eventually nurture an individual:

We always have visions before a thing is made real. When we realize that although the vision is real, it is not real in us, then is the time that Satan comes in with his temptations, and we are apt to say it is no use to go on. Instead of the vision becoming real, there has come the valley of humiliation.

God gives us the vision, then He takes us down to the valley to batter us into the shape of the vision, and it is in the valley that so many of us faint and give way. Every vision will be made real if we will have patience. Think of the enormous leisure of God! He is never in a hurry. We are always in such a frantic hurry. In the light of the glory of the vision we go forth to do things, but the vision is not real in us yet; and God has to take us into the valley and put us through fires and floods to batter us into shape, until we get to the place where He can trust us with the veritable reality.

Ever since we had the vision God has been at work, getting us into the shape of the ideal, and over and over again we escape from His hand and try to batter ourselves into our own shape. The vision is not a castle in the air, but a vision of what God wants you to be. Let Him put you on His wheel and whirl you as He likes, and as sure as God is God and you are you, you will turn out exactly in accordance with the vision. Don't lose heart in the process. If you have ever had the vision of God, you may try as you like to be satisfied on a lower level, but God will never let you. My determination is to be my Utmost for His Highest.[4]

[4] Oswald Chambers, *My Utmost for His Highest*, revised edition (Grand Rapids, MI: Discovery House Publishers, 2008), p. 188.

After my daughter, Christina, was born in 1991, Gwen and I had opportunities to grow deeper in the things of God. I felt that God was leading us in a season to be nurtured and prospered by Him, but Gwen had many fears and unfilled dreams of her own.

I remember Gwen describing my personality at that time of our lives. She said, "It is like living with someone that you'd known for a very long time who has suddenly turned 180 degrees and living with this person is an unfamiliar place for me. I am having a challenging time living with him and in accepting his personal choices and lifestyle."

I love it when God puts a "suddenly" into my life! Gwen was right. I had changed radically! There was no going back to religion. (The root word for religion is bondage.) Now I wanted to daily walk in the "River of God," which meant to be immersed in God's mighty flowing, cleansing, and redeeming water of life! This living presence of God is such a release and refreshment to my spirit, soul, and body. As an overflow, I desire to see the Holy Spirit tangibly touch others with His presence.

In the early 1990s, when the tension and the conflict began to spiritually erupt between us as a couple, I knew that Gwen was struggling. Gwen would no longer physically or mentally be a part of my artistic and ministry interests, musical career, or destiny. She would exit stage right out of my life.

"GOD CONNECTIONS" FORMED WITH CCM ARTISTS

In 1992, I was invited to create, work on, and produce a national television pilot program entitled *Break Thru TV* in a partnership with a Christian television network in Canada. But before I get ahead of myself, let me go back a bit. I want to share the outcome of God-moments and the release of such blessing and favour.

God opened the doors for me to jump-start a new opportunity in Christian broadcasting, beginning with my first interview with Sandi Patty on September 12, 1992. Then in March 1993, I attended the Gospel Music Association's convention and Dove Awards ceremony in Nashville, Tennessee. There I recorded on film many hours of interviews with some of Gospel music's finest artists.

Before the concept for *Break Thru TV* was even created, I enjoyed a specific creative period and artistic expression—ADHD and all! At that time, my workload included connecting, meeting, and interviewing all the CCM's musical artists that came to London, Ontario. What I lacked in actual television production experience I learned from being in the right environment around experienced production folk. In other words, being in the right place at the right time around the right people. These were indeed God moments! Having developed my skills base via cable television, I knew immediately when *Break Thru TV* came into being that this was something I could do very well!

The Word of God says not to despise small beginnings. My experience began with cable television and some very primitive equipment for editing. While it was a small beginning, it offered tremendous opportunity to develop my writing, interviewing skills, and production techniques. I worked on a cable gospel program called *Sounds of Praise*, a Christian music program hosted by the late Ivan Hutton of London. Ivan was a pioneer in the field of using film clips of live nature settings blended with audio sound tracks. Using a Super-8 video camera, we produced three shows with Christian family content.

Ivan's program ministered to many senior shut-ins, and he would receive many thank you letters or phone calls of gratitude. Through concerts and even outside bandstand events, Ivan helped to develop and encourage many local artists in their ministries. These events featured artists who had appeared on his program. Ivan and I had the opportunity together to produce a backstage interview program with Sandi Patty.

Through a series of events and networking with a few Nashville publicists, I was given the assignment as an interviewer/broadcaster on location. As I mentioned earlier, my first ever on-camera television interview was with Grammy and Dove Award winning artist Sandi Patty at Canada's Wonderland. Being given this opportunity to interview Sandi was truly a God moment! This wet-behind-the-ears and novice broadcaster-musician was so thrilled and honoured to interview my mentor, Sandi Patty. Sandi Patty and her management team represented the finest Christian musicians, artists, and producers from the Nashville area.

Many American CCM artists and their ministries had already come to Canada. Without the availability of daily Christian radio, it was difficult and very expensive for American ministries to tour in Canada. In addition to opening all those doors for many Christian music artists, God blessed me with a wonderful time, connection, and great rapport with Sandi.

Sandi Patty and me connecting for my first CCM interview in Toronto. It was a wonderful experience in 1992. (ECG Photo Collection)

During this initial interview, Sandi was having an enjoyable time talking to me about her project in 1993, "Le Voyage," which eventually became a full faith-filled musical production. As an artist and a singer, I knew that this project had highly creative and rich lyrical context. These cuts from the CD were similar in design, style, and lyrical content to a Broadway musical in the vein of another favourite composer, Stephen Sondheim. Responding to my questions, Sandi freely opened and shared more about how the meaningful lyrics and background of the story created the potential for the future evolution of the full musical. The concept was based on the best-selling Christian books *Pilgrim's Progress* and *Hinds' Feet on High Places*. Of all of Sandi's varied recordings, this album is still one of my favourites.

It was getting closer and closer to show time, and Sandi stopped the interview. She asked us if we could stay for the entire show and then pick up the remaining interview questions afterward. I was dumbfounded. Of course my answer was "Yes! Whatever will work for you." Sandi's opening act was Mark Lowry. I remember standing in the wings of the theatre, watching and listening to Sandi sing and minister one of her trademark songs, "We Shall Behold Him." I pinched myself to see if I was really backstage, hearing that wonderful God-centred vocal artist ministering to a crowd of more than two thousand people. Even today, those wonderful memories still excite me and fill me with joy. To think that God would allow me, a novice broadcaster, to connect and begin a strong friendship with Sandi that continues today.

A few days after the interview, I spoke to Sandi's agent in Nashville. I asked, "Has Sandi ever started an interview and then asked the interviewer if they could finish the interview after the end of the show?"

"No, that had never happened before."

Sandi Patty and me in November 2016, Michigan venue, on her "Forever Grateful Tour" (ECG Photo Collection)

With that, I knew God had blessed me with a genuine connection with Sandi Patty.

Over the last twenty years, Sandi and I have connected via email. She has been a great friend, mentor, and recently professor to me. In the summer of 2016, I graduated from Mid-America Christian University's Christian Worship Arts and Leadership Program (CWAL) via their online program. Sandi Patty is the founder and "artist in residence" to this program. You can stay in touch with Sandi's personal engagements or new projects at www.sandipatty.com.

In 2016–2017, Sandi Patty announced her retirement from recording and touring after a career of nearly forty years in the Gospel music industry. Sandi presently serves as "artist in residence" at Crossings Community Church in Oklahoma City. She is a great communicator, writer, and storyteller, as well as worship and music mentor to the next generation of CCM artists and worship leaders.

From Southern Ontario to GMA in Nashville in the mid 1990s, I have interviewed many Christian music legends. The extensive list includes: Steven Curtis Chapman, Ralph Carmichael, (composer/arranger and conductor of the Young Messiah Tour), Rick Cua, Phil Driscoll, Bryan Duncan, Steve Green, Mark Lowry, Cindy Morgan, and Randy Stonehill. In 1995, with the late Jim Leek, music director of 1250 Joy radio, I researched artists' bios and produced radio interviews with well-known CCM artists, such as Cliff Barrows, Music Director of the Toronto Billy Graham Crusade, Steven Curtis Chapman, the late Andrae Crouch, and Michael W. Smith.

I remember being in a very difficult and emotional place in January of 1993. After the success of the Sandi Patty interview, new broadcasting opportunities started to come my way, and I was making valuable connections within the Nashville music community. I had some tough career decisions to make for my future and the wellbeing of my family. Should I move in a new direction toward a full-time salaried position as a Christian music broadcaster/producer, or stay on course toward becoming a full-time arts administrator, my dream job? Working as an apprentice in sales, marketing, and fundraising duties for Orchestra London Canada

(OLC) gave me tremendous skills that I now use every day; however, working for this organization part-time meant a low salary. Needing additional income, I held a second part-time job with Eaton's department store. During the downturn of economic conditions in the 1980s and early 1990s, a full-time arts position in the performing arts industry was extremely difficult to secure. In the midst of my trying personal issues, having the opportunity to develop my interests and skills through cable TV and video kept me sane.

After the Patty interview, I longed to use my talents and skills in Christian broadcasting full-time. I sought God, and I remember that as I read the Word, God would speak to me, showing me a step-by-step plan and vision. But it had touchy conditions. If I were willing to walk with Him in faith, then I would experience unspeakable joy and begin to fulfill my destiny.

I prayed sans ceasing for weeks. Before I stepped out in faith, I consulted with close friends and pastors. From the initial stages of this project, I felt that God's blessings to me were confirmed. I had the assurance that He was in this venture. Having networked with these A-list Christian artists was confirmation to me. God was indeed opening doors for me and my talents; however, only He would develop my future career as a Christian music broadcaster/producer. The only other person with whom I could share these dreams, longings, and intimate artistic feelings was Grandma Violet. When the opportunity to interview Sandi Patty was present, Violet knew that God was totally involved. When I asked if she would lend me the needed funds for ongoing television production and interviewing twenty-three CCM artists, Grandma Violet said that she would pray about it.

My future producing this pilot program could be the beginnings of a potential full-time career. Violet did pray about it. My mother tried to talk her out of financially supporting me; however, Grandma told me later that the Lord wouldn't let her sleep until she agreed to be obedient and release the funds. Afterwards, when Violet had been obedient, she told me that she had such peace about this project. She also said that the Lord had blessed her with one of the deepest sleeps she'd ever experienced. The next morning, Grandma wrote me a cheque for the agreed amount. But Grandma Violet wasn't to be alone in this venture. My parents were also kept awake all night. They sensed the Lord directing them to lend me the remaining costs of my travel, accommodations, hotel, and food.

The time came when Gwen and I discussed the options available for getting this project off the ground and for me living and boarding with my grandmother for a brief period. As a couple, we had made a verbal agreement: she would support our young family for six months, and then we would evaluate our next steps. Gwen and I had prayed and verbally agreed on this temporary separation. I thought that this project would prove to be a valuable experience for our relationship, as I was stepping out in faith.

I believed that the Holy Spirit was leading me into prosperity and a positive career move. All indications were that a full-fledged television series would be doable if the objectives were met in producing an excellent television pilot program, developing an audience, and marketing for this program. At that time, the vision for a new career would be realized. As far as I knew, we were both on board.

At the beginning of each interview, the entire production team prayed together and invited the Holy Spirit right into the sessions. We prayed over the television equipment and blessed the crew to function in their roles. Some of these artists were so blessed when we prayed for God's presence. Through the Lord's blessing and strength, and a hefty dose of adrenaline, I completed twenty-three interviews with these various CCM artists in just two days. The venture had successfully launched! Fulfilled vision was right around the corner.

CHAPTER THIRTEEN
PRAISE BANDS, JESUS ROCK, AND CONTEMPORARY WORSHIP

My encounters with a few of the artists have been more than amazing. Without a doubt, these are contacts that God arranged, and this was a very blessed time for me. When these "connections" started to open for me, I was in a whirlwind! Here I was, this "ADHD guy," putting these interviews together, working in media, radio, and television, as well as producing this project and loving it all! I have also included many of these artists' websites, should you want to know more about their ministries. Many of them are good friends to me.

Nashville is a media town for both country music and the Christian music industry. I enjoyed completing the entire twenty-seven artist research packets on each artist and listening to and critiquing their project or CD. I received a fee per artist for the interviews that I conducted in Nashville. The rest of the initial start-up costs were covered by the funds borrowed from my parents and from my grandmother. Much of the post-production funds needed to complete this program would need to come from potential sponsors.

One of my Canadian TV crew colleagues commented on my style of interviewing. "You have a very similar style to that of the late Brian Linehan." What a great compliment! Brian Linehan was also a Hamilton, Ontario native. Known in Canada and internationally as the "interviewer to the Hollywood Stars," he made his living from both radio and television. Due to his incredible research and ability to obtain uncommon knowledge on these celebrities, Brian had a great rapport with Hollywood legends. Brian's program, *City Lights*, was a favourite of mine to watch in the 1970s and 1990s. I would listen to the way that Brian phrased a question. His style of interviewing didn't seem canned to me. Sadly, Brian died in 2005 of non-Hodgkin's lymphoma.

When we were filming the CCM Nashville interviews, I applied the Linehan approach. I had prepared and knew the background histories, musical interests, new CDs launched, and the "faith-filled testimonies" of the artists I was soon to interview. I later would build relationships with these artists or their management companies. I tried to avoid asking the standard "canned" questions that a typical interviewer would ask. I asked these artists about their careers and about their spiritual walk with the Lord.

Prior to the GMA event, I had the wonderful opportunity in November of 1992 to interview Ralph Carmichael and CCM Legend, Randy Stonehill. Ralph had been a musical legend for many years when he and his partner, Kurt Kaiser, wrote *Tell It like It Is*, a 1970s Christian musical that included rich and devotional songs such as "Pass it On," "He's Everything to Me," and "Master Designer."

In the 1950s, Ralph had worked with legends such as Bing Crosby, Nat King Cole, Peggy Lee, Ella Fitzgerald, Jack Jones, and Rosemary Clooney on many projects at Capital Records in Hollywood. Ralph's original orchestral arrangements included musicians from *I Love Lucy*, and he later composed scores for golden-era TV programs such as *Bonanza* and *The Danny Kaye Show*. Ralph was also one of the original artists to establish his own Christian publishing company, Lexicon Music, and later Light Records, launching careers such artists as Andrae Crouch, The Winans, and Bryan Duncan. This recording label is now a part of Word Records. Ralph has also composed many film scores for Billy Graham's World-Wide Pictures.

Ralph was on a tour in Ontario with David Boyer, a big-band gospel singer. Ralph was conducting his orchestra with his innovative jazz and big band arrangements of hymns and standard gospel ballads. When interviewing him, I asked, "Ralph, you're known as the Dean of Christian Contemporary Christian Music. What is God saying to you regarding current trends in CCM today?" That question primed the pump for some deep conversation between us.

"Let me tell you," he said. "Life is a cycle and the rediscovery of simple and basic things. Recently, I've re-examined redemption's contract. What is my part and what is God's part? For being so brief, my part is very tough. My part is two words—trust and obey! I dwell on this statement and trust in this to keep my life simple. Through death, Christ paid the debt of sin for me. Through His life, He breaks the power of sin for me. If I obey. I think the best thing that I can do for young musicians coming along is to represent that simple truth. It's neither fancy nor complicated, is it? It is the truth.

"If I can stay steady with that truth," he continued, "then I won't be blown hither and yonder with the tensions or the politics of music and its changes. Years and years ago, I fought for the privilege of experimenting and changing the contemporary Christian music genres. Now as I'm getting older, the thing I have to be careful about is that I not be critical of the changes yet to come in the industry. I don't have to participate in or even like all of the changes that will take place. It's very unlikely that I will use midi the way they compose music today. I see a lot of that happening, and that's fine. I'm rather old fashioned; I write my music on score paper, which then goes to a copyist and ends up on a music stand.

"I remember when we couldn't use the word 'rock.' I played a rhythmic beat such as dong-chic, dong, dong-chic-dong, dong in a Sunday morning service at a West Coast church. I felt like the walls were going to collapse on me! One of the deacons of the church was taking me back to the airport. He said, 'You have sinned this morning, and we all know it!' But you see, we won that battle! Today when I go into churches all over North America, I see that they have their own drum sets. I remember in the early years when drum sets had to be hidden behind a curtain or in a walled-off area. I was on the front battle lines for experimentation and for opening new vistas of musical possibilities. Now as I am coming to the end of the race, the last thing that I want to do is show any form of censorship. I encourage all experimentation, and I believe that 'things' are neither good nor evil; depending upon the use to which they are put, 'things' become instruments of good or evil.

"It's hard to believe that what we participate freely in today was suspect for more than sixty years. Barely seventy years ago, even the radio was considered the devil's little black box. My father was involved as a radio preacher, and he was severely criticized for being on the radio. My first television program in which I participated could not be identified with the actual Christian college I was attending. Going even farther back in history, the printing press implemented the idea of mass producing portions of God's Word—but it was prohibited. Singing in harmony was once considered very worldly! When isn't it all about how God can use all of these media and musical elements for His glory?

"All of these new things are just things … neither good nor evil. My part in today's entire music scene is to hold steady and encourage people. Proverbs tells us that wisdom and understanding are close to God's heart. In my opinion, if a talented young person would spend time reading Proverbs, meditating on God's Word, and then proceed with musical experimentation and interpretation, God would bless their efforts."[5]

From Ralph Carmichael's biography, *He's Everything to Me*, we read:

Carmichael has written "every kind of music there is." But you'll never know what kind of music he likes personally. "That's not important," he says. "What is important is the fact that music must communicate the gospel. God has never promised to bless any musical form, only to bless His Word. I don't know how many

---

[5] Walker, W. Ian, Interview with Ralph Carmichael. *Break Thru TV,* WIW, November, 1992.

notes I've got left in my pencil, but I want them used to glorify God and present His message to the World." [6]

During my interview with Ralph, we talked about his three-year commitment to the Young Messiah Tour as music director to produce the contemporary version of Handel's *Young Messiah* composition. These tours involved many CCM artists, with individual choirs and orchestras from each local venue. Spending precious time with Ralph Carmichael was such an honour and a pleasure. I couldn't have asked for a more wonderful Christmas gift than to meet and interview Ralph during the fall holiday season of 1992.

With Ralph Carmichael, one of my "heroes of the faith," and Dave Boyer.
(ECG Photo Collection)

During the fall of 1992 and before my team went to Nashville, I had the wonderful opportunity to interview legendary CCM artist Randy Stonehill in Toronto. As I mentioned previously, I had known of Randy's career since the mid-seventies, and here I was interviewing this CCM legend. I was such a neophyte. At that time he was a twenty-five-year veteran.

---

[6] "Inductees Archive: Ralph Carmichael," *Gospel Music Hall of Fame.* http://hof.doveawards.com/speaker-lineup/ralph-carmichael/ (accessed April 2, 2018).

Randy was very amicable as we chatted about his current (1992) project. The meat of the interview concerned the early years of his involvement with the Jesus Movement music of the 1970s. I asked him about his early connections with Keith Green and the late Larry Norman.

"In the early days of the Jesus music," he started, "people like myself, Larry Norman, and Chuck Girard (of the 'Hondell's,' produced by Brian Wilson) were doing what came naturally. We were talking about the passion of our new-found faith and trying to articulate that with the tools that we'd been given, which was our love of rock and roll. That was our language.

"Some people within the church, and even outside of the church walls, saw that this music was very genuine, and it seemed to be propelled by the Spirit. God was using it! Regarding our new style of rock and roll in Christian music, the more old-school, conservative church thinkers said, 'Wait a minute here,' and wanted to throw the baby out with the bathwater. They had seen all of the damage done to the church in the sixties and gave rock and roll all the blame. They said it was the fault of that music and 'how dare you bring it into the church!' Or 'how dare you cheapen this holy gospel in this shoddy package and or framework?

Connecting with Randy Stonehill, one of the originals of the Jesus Music Movement, 1992 (ECG Photo Collection)

"The press (who don't care as long as they get viewers or sell newspapers), saw that something was going on here. We were controversial, and they just said, 'We don't understand it, but we know that it's news.' Suddenly, we were in *Time* magazine and *Newsweek*. And they called it the Jesus Movement.

"That title cracks me up, as I think that this movement actually started centuries before. Larry Norman said, 'Don't call it church music and don't call it rock and roll. Call it 'Jesus Rock!' That is something we all can understand.' The press ran with it. 'We'll stamp that music Jesus Rock, yes sir!' We all started from there."

I continued my questions. "What are your impressions of the Christian contemporary music and the marketing of it?"

"During the last thirty years, I've seen both the good and the unsettling things in the church with this genre of music. As people learned how to produce state-of-the-art recordings, I saw this music diversify, and a lot of talent rise to the surface. I've seen the church embrace this genre to an extent—but I've also seen and experienced the undermining of the heart of what it started out to be. I find this very troubling.

"The fact is, the church is the primary record buying audience for this genre of music. Christian record companies specifically target that audience market. The church is starting to dictate how real you can get … in other words, what you can and cannot do! I have seen this take place in Christian radio as well. It's like they are stating, 'This is ours,' and in a passive mindset, settle for 'don't make me think, don't give me too much passion and edge, and lastly, don't get too preachy!'

"Wait a minute! If anybody has a responsibility for self-exploration and some type of internal revolution taking place, and to be talking about or challenging ourselves on these issues, it should be the Christians! Christians are human beings like anybody else, and we're sinners. By and large, we prefer not to rock the boat! Essentially, we say just give me some happy music or make me feel the victory message, and if you're going to play rock, make those drums loud! Then, if you want me to respond in the spiritual environment of the moment, you're going to have to soften the music to something very sweet and comforting. Otherwise, we as a church body are not going to receive it!

"I think that this man-made mentality undermines the impact of what God intends for this type of music for His specific place and time. The new challenge for me and for other artists like me is to keep our vision and keep our edge, for these are complacent times."[7]

This time spent with Randy was such a musical CCM history lesson for me! You can learn more about Randy's amazing career and his on-going ministry projects at www.randystonehill.com.

While I was attending the Dove Awards in 1993, I sat in my assigned seat and watched how the GMA produced the show. This invitation was my first Nashville experience backstage, and I congratulated the artists who had won awards. That evening, Steven Curtis Chapman had broken all of the previous records for the Dove Awards (winning six awards for his album *The Great Adventure*, which is now twenty-five years old).

Previously, I had commented to Steven that I was looking forward to the GMA convention and Dove Awards. I would also have some time to be a tourist in Music City. With many Dove awards in his hands, and after chatting with some friends, he turned to me and said, "Ian, good to see you. Did you have a fun time in Nashville and at the Dove's?"

Connecting with Steven Curtis Chapman in Nashville, TN in 1993

[7] Walker, W. Ian. Interview with Randy Stonehill. *Break Thru TV.* 1992.

I was totally speechless! Steven remembered my name and then asked how my stay was in Nashville. That Steven had welcomed this stranger to the industry and Nashville was another example of pure southern hospitality.

Steven is an outstanding artist and humanitarian. Just being around Steven is such a humbling experience. You can learn more about Steven's passion for life, his music, and his ministry at: www.stevencurtischapman.com

Interviewing Mark Lowry was an experience! Knowing Mark's style and humour could make you break up at any time. He is known for his involvement with the *Gaither Homecoming* television programs. We are both artists, and we have both dealt with our ADHD disorders. Now when I email Mark, I remind him of our connections and that we are alumni of the ADHD Club. In the spring of 1994, Mark was in Southern Ontario. I was still working on the pre-production of the pilot of *Break Thru TV*. We connected again and had a great reunion luncheon. You can stay in touch with Mark at www.marklowry.com

Taking a breather with Mark Lowry in Nashville in 1993.
(ECG Photo Collection)

I grew up in the 1980s listening to Sandi Patty, Larnelle Harris, Phil Driscoll, and Steve Green. I was very excited to meet and record an interview with Steve Green. As a singer, I already knew a lot about Steve's background and his conversion to the Lord. To this very day his tenor voice is so rich and pure. He would sing acapella in many of his concerts. When singing the hymn "A Mighty Fortress Is Our God," he would go up a semi-tone after each verse, concluding the arrangement with a major high C note that would bring the house down.

During our conversation, I asked Steve where he was personally and professionally with the Lord. His answer moved me. Steve was spending enormous amounts of time memorizing the New Testament, because he felt that he didn't have a solid command of the Word. Steve said that he wanted to be able to evangelize with the gospel even more. We talked about his role as a father, husband, and now grandfather and as a tenor gospel music singer. He commented: "However, at the end of the day, I hope to be remembered for being a good provider for my family, a great dad to my children, and an excellent husband to my wife." [8]

I was truly blessed by having spent some God time with Steve Green. In my opinion, he is one of God's true runners of the faith. To stay in touch with Steve Green, you can contact him at: www.stevegreenministries.org.

As I met and became friendly with these established artists and celebrities, their warmth and acceptance of me as a fellow-traveller helped to fan the flame of a dawning awareness that, despite the ADHD that often made me feel like I was in a fog and disorganized, when I was focused and organized, I could indeed achieve so much! My contact with and acceptance by these established figures was providing me with the momentum to combat my ADHD.

---

[8] Walker, W. Ian. Interview with Steve Green. *Break Thru TV.* April 1993.

CHAPTER FOURTEEN
HEROES OF FAITH, UP CLOSE AND PERSONAL

As far back as 1948, my mother, Doreen, participated in the early beginnings of Youth for Christ events in Toronto. She sang in what would later become Billy Graham's future ministry—the Campus Crusade Choir. In my teen years, as a family we would attend Billy Graham's Greater Toronto Area crusades. During a time of pre-crusade preparation in 1995, Billy Graham and his teammates, Cliff Burrows and George Beverley Shea, were at the Sky-Dome (now known as Rogers Centre) in Toronto. I was invited and given press credentials to the crusade and all media events, including a press conference at the venue with Dr. Graham and others in Christian media.

Billy Graham seemed tired. I wondered if there was anything medically wrong. I dismissed the thought, assuming that it was probably jet lag. I prepared a question for the BGEA media staff on June 6, 1995: "What was the ministry's focus toward CCM style of music, and what was their mission or motive in doing so?" Little did I know that I asked this question right to Billy Graham himself. Billy first responded to the question and then asked for some feedback from Michael W. Smith, who could give an updated response.

I was amazed, shocked, and impressed that Billy Graham would speak directly to me and answer my question. Once again, I felt God's favour. Here I was a novice broadcaster/producer, dialoguing face to face with Billy Graham. After the press conference, Dr. Graham came around and greeted those who'd asked him questions. He thanked me personally for my question and then he shook my hand. Wouldn't you know that I didn't bring my camera with me that day? I had personally met, chatted with, and shook hands with the legendary Billy Graham. My parents were thrilled!

On June 7, 1995, I was again invited with other press to attend the famous conference in which Billy Graham collapsed. He would not preach at all during the Toronto Crusade. This press conference occurred just before noon that day, and Billy Graham was not physically or emotionally prepared to give a public address. He didn't want to disappoint his Toronto hosts in not attending this pre-crusade media event. He was present against the wisdom and the wishes of his doctor. A few minutes into this speech, Dr. Graham regretfully said that he had to stop his speech, as he was about to collapse, and if someone would call for an ambulance he would be most appreciative. The next thing we saw was Billy Graham slowly positioning himself to lie down on the floor of the platform, waiting for medical help.

This experience was totally overwhelming to all the media assembled in that hotel room! We all were in shock. The Christians immediately started to pray for Dr. Graham, that he would get the immediate attention that he needed ... oh yes, and that the crusade would continue as planned! Due to his health, and after this attempted public appearance, Billy Graham had no choice. His doctors would not allow him to participate in the Toronto crusades. The focus of the meetings then shifted to the pinch-hitter, Canadian evangelist Dr. Ralph Bell. Even then, thousands of new decisions were made for Christ during these Toronto meetings.

Having had personal contact with the late Jim Leek (music director of Joy 1250 Radio in Oakville, Ontario), I called him immediately and reported this event "live" to him on the air. We discussed Billy Graham's collapse. That was my first experience of live reporting to CJMR radio. God was truly preparing me for many open doors of blessings as a future broadcaster. My job was to be available and to be prepared.

I had the opportunity to interview the late Cliff Barrows, Billy Graham's devoted faithful friend, worship leader, and producer. Later in his career, Cliff Barrows became the music director for all of Billy Graham Evangelistic Association's (BGEA) musical needs. I asked Cliff about being prepared for the job that he was initially given. His response was honest and forthright:

"I didn't have any formal musical training or education. I had been a band leader who could write and arrange music; however, God used my simple gifts to His glory, and it has been a privilege for me to be associated with the BGEA for over fifty years … just being a support to Billy however he could use me."[9]

The late Dr. Billy Graham, who passed away at ninety-nine years of age, was the last remaining member of the five godly men who first stood together to start this ministry in the early 1950s. His legacy is enormous all around the world! Even today, I am so blessed as I reflect on the fact that I was able to meet Dr. Graham and have a few minutes with him.

After one of the evenings of worship at the crusade, I witnessed two incredible God experiences—one with gospel singer/composer Andrae Crouch, and the other with CCM entertainers DC Talk. Jim Leek and I were waiting for an interview with Andrae; however, Andrae and his worship teams of fine singers were still worshipping backstage after ministering at the crusade. Sweetly in the presence of the Lord, they continued to lift their voices in songs of praise. I had never experienced such an anointing of pure praise and worship. It was like fine gold dust hovering and shimmering all over the room! Many members of the press were waiting to connect with Andrae. The praise and worship from Andrae and his singers gave us a little taste of Heaven—right here on earth!

God had heard my prayers. As a young boy, I had read Andrae's autobiography, *Through It All*, and learned that he had suffered from

---

[9] Walker, W. Ian. Interview with Cliff Barrows. *Break Thru TV.* 1995.

dyslexia as a boy and that God had healed him. In early January 2015, Andrae Crouch passed away at the age of seventy-two. His music and gospel catalogue, plus his legendary down-to-earth attitude, will never be forgotten—especially by me! I was so blessed to have met him. In that precious God moment, I told Andrae what an influence both he and his book had on me in the early years of dealing with my ADHD and its challenges.

During one of the evenings at the crusade, I was supposed to have interviewed Michael W. Smith, known to his closest friends as "Smitty." Just as he was finishing a sound check, I was introduced to him. Unfortunately, there was a last-minute change to Michael's schedule. Still backstage in the green room, Jim and I were waiting for Smitty.

Then, God changed our timetable and in walked the hottest new contemporary rock group—DC Talk, recipients of many Grammy and Dove awards. Because of this change in Smitty's schedule, we were afforded some up-close-and-personal time with Kevin Max, Toby McKeehan (Toby Mac), and Michael Tait.

We met the boys in a relaxed moment and gave them some advice as to the best spots to visit in Toronto. Since CCM music and radio weren't as popular here as in the USA, these artists could walk around Toronto totally unnoticed. They loved that! I chatted with one of DC Talk's bodyguards, and it turned out that he was also their bass player. He was very friendly! I asked him, "Do the boys have a pastor or spiritual leader with them to keep them accountable to their calling while they tour?"

He told me that he was a part of their spiritual covering and that they spent time together in prayer and Bible study while they were on the road. His conversation with us reassured me that, despite all the fame and worldwide adulation that these young men attracted, they were grounded securely to the firm foundation of Jesus Christ.

Within a brief span of two years, these amazing experiences and contacts with some of gospel music's artists took place. I was excited and thrilled, but I must admit I wasn't prepared. These events and meetings with well-known artists meant a level of spiritual warfare that was new to me. Unprepared for the many roadblocks, I experienced moments of deep depression punctuated by overwhelming emotional highs and then lows. I was also dealing with a lot of personal family issues at this time.

I had no idea how hard I would have to work just to focus my eyes and ears totally on trusting God. I was very committed to seeing this project completed from A–Z. The faith walk was certainly riddled with emotional minefields. Many people initially were interested in supporting me financially with the *Break Thru TV* project, but then they didn't come through. I spent a lot of time on my knees, fasting, praying, and asking God for His presence to make sure that my motives were pure in continuing this project before Him.

My dear friend, Nancy Honeytree-Miller, has an amazing song called "Pioneer" that describes this pioneering stage of my faith walk. To some degree, I am even today in that early frontier pioneer stage. There is always something new to try, someplace else to go, another hurdle to jump, and another intersection to navigate. At the same time, I only want to hear God's voice and His direction for my life. These lyrics are very true to what it feels like to be a pioneer.

My desire is to be totally used of God as salt and light for today and for future generations; however, God chooses to use my life, my whole heart's desire is to be involved in creating family programming that will glorify God.

Connecting with Nancy Honeytree Miller, in 2006, after taping with YCFN on the 100 Huntley Street *Christmas program (ECG Photo Collection)*

"Pioneer"

CHORUS

Pioneer, pioneer,
Keep pressing onward, beyond your fear;
Only the Father goes before you
To your own frontier.
You're a pioneer
Uncharted wilderness stretches beyond you,
And you thrive on going where no one has gone;
Still it gets lonely when darkness deepens,
So sing by the fire until the dawn …

CHORUS

You travel light, you travel alone,
And when you arrive, nobody knows,
But the Father in Heaven, He's glad you can go,
For those who come after you will need the road.

CHORUS

What you have done others will do,
Bigger and better and faster than you,
But you can't look back, no you gotta keep pressing through,
There's a wilderness pathway, and it's calling you.
Calling you, calling you clear,
So keep pressing onward, you can't stay here;
Only the Father goes before you
To your own frontier.
You're a pioneer.

Nancy Honeytree Millar C 1993 Oak Table Publishing Inc. /ASCAP

CHAPTER FIFTEEN
A LIVING NIGHTMARE, A PERSISTENT DREAM

Gwen Woods, a young, self-conscious girl, not only sang in our high school choir but was a good musician overall. A member of the local Youth Symphony Orchestra, Gwen was also interested in choral music. She was an active member in her home church choir. Her personal involvement with these two musical organizations was very appealing. With musical credentials like mine, she was high on my preference list for my future spouse. In hindsight, I didn't know the first thing about how to seek God about His selection for my life partner.

At seventeen, we enjoyed being together, which later developed into a loving, youthful relationship. We became high school sweethearts. Right from the beginning of our relationship until its very end, we needed each other emotionally. Gwen was one year older that me; however, she was three years ahead of me in high school when we began our relationship. I was in Grade nine.

We did all the things that teenage couples do: attend dances, eat pizza, and have special places to hang out together. My upbringing and interests meant we would also be at various church services, youth events, and coffee houses. Many times I would be asked to perform my own songs at these events.

Gwen and I had been together as a young couple for eight years by the time she completed her BA in Music Education. I was planning to complete my second year in music at the University of Western Ontario (UWO). We broke up, but only for a brief time. Neither of us could face the fact that we should not be together. In January 1983, Gwen gave me an ultimatum: "Either we get engaged when I graduate in 1983, or we go our separate ways." I asked Gwen to marry me that spring. Sadly, I wish that I had listened to that inner voice telling me to wait.

I had difficulty focusing and struggled with time-management issues, combined with other ADHD symptoms. It was already hard for me to have a part-time job combined with school studies; however, I had to work. It was not an option. I chose to marry Gwen and thought that together as a normal couple we could overcome all temporary obstacles for the next year or two until I could complete my BA.

Gwen had all the right attributes that I was looking for in a spouse. Only in hindsight could I see that if I had looked closer at the areas where we didn't match, I might have noticed many red flags. Just a few weeks before the wedding, three people from within my family and circle of close friends tried to tell me that our personalities did not match, and that perhaps we should call off the wedding. Of course, I thought that their observations were wrong. Had I truly sought God and listened to the prophetic counsel around me, I am sure that my life would have been considerably different.

A summer wedding was planned and, wouldn't you know it, it was one of the hottest days of the summer of 1984! One of the wonderful things about being with other music majors was that you could recruit your friends to be your vocal entertainment. I had many great friends who made up the wedding chorale. My long-term friend, Brainerd Blyden-Taylor, acted as our conductor of the chorale. He is now the founder and artistic director of the internationally known Nathaniel Dett Chorale.

My dear friend, Alpha Omega (Gonzalez) Cruz-Lopez (my Tanglewood harpist friend), came to the wedding with her boyfriend and with "Momma Gonzalez" all the way from Houston, Texas. Alpha sang in the chorale, and how I wish that I'd had the extra money to rent a harp for Alpha so that she could have played at our wedding.

You would have thought that Cinderella and her prince had entered a happy and fulfilled life taking up residence in a magic castle; however, within five years, the illusion of a fairy-tale marriage began to shatter. It wasn't until almost ten years later that I realized how our mutual interests were seriously different. It was obvious. We could NOT be together.

Toward the end of our marriage and after I had that incredible experience of growing deeper with God in 1992, I was being healed of many emotional ailments, such as depression, low self-esteem, and lack of purpose. By the mid-1990s, Gwen and I were growing apart. I didn't see the cracks in our foundation until I later stepped out in faith toward starting my solo broadcasting and music ministry. We once shared a common interest in Classical, choral, and contemporary Christian music.

IMPACT AND INSIGHTS—DEALING WITH DIFFICULT RELATIONSHIPS FROM AN ADHD PERSPECTIVE

From my perspective, Gwen needed to be in control of everything. Perhaps with my ADHD issues, it was easier for her to do so. This control included our finances and attempting to control me, her husband. We had several heated discussions between our fifth and eighth wedding anniversary about moving back to the Greater Toronto Area for work for me! We both had grown apart. I sensed the laser-like voice of the Holy Spirit speaking and showing me that, in the future, this relationship would be over. I was in shock and resisted. I remained hopeful that we could reconcile our differences.

Only after we had been separated for a year, during the filming and production of the *Break Thru TV* project, did I realize how much I had been drowning in this relationship and marriage. There were "heated discussions" about my TV project and our future, our finances, and moving back to the Toronto area that just didn't seem to get resolved. Combined with my ADHD symptoms, I felt my destiny had been suppressed. After having that supernatural experience in 1992, everything shifted, and I knew in my spirit that I needed to follow God's call on my life.

Alpha Cruz-Lopez emailed me recently and asked: "What really went wrong with you two?" Because she was a trusted friend, I gave her my version of the story. She emailed me back, saying further: "I often wondered what had happened to the most beautiful Christian couple that I had known." I was totally shocked by her response! I personally believed that we were being groomed as the Lord's servants and worshippers; however, once anger, bitterness, jealousy, resentment, and the competition for the affection of our daughter entered in, there was nothing left of the initial cornerstone of our marriage. Despite some solid counselling, Gwen later admitted to me and our counsellors that, for her, the marriage was basically over as early as 1989.

THE BIRTH OF CHRISTINA

Just before Christina was born in spring of 1991, Grandma Violet wrote to me about her excitement over being involved with the preparations for her second great-grandchild:

"I think that your mom is really looking forward to the baby coming. She is not the emotional type. When the birth happens, she will probably 'shout it from the rooftops,' as the saying goes. I am sure when the baby comes she will love it. I have been busy knitting and crocheting. I have made a shawl, set of baby clothes, booties, and bonnet, and I am making another set. I expect that you are really getting excited. I pray that the baby will be healthy and will have a safe delivery. Are you going to be there at the birthing? They didn't do that in our day. Things have really changed!"

I have many wonderful memories and pictures of Christina as a baby and toddler. When I learned that Gwen was pregnant, I began to speak blessings and prayed over this developing child every night. I constantly talked to the baby. I wanted this child to know my voice! Gwen had a difficult labour with Christina, who was delivered in a breech position. We had decided on two names—Rebecca or Christina.

Four generations of Helmkay-Walker family in 1991
(Walker Family Photo Collection)

Seeing our precious daughter for the first time with her light skin, delicate features, Zoë personality, and her alert blue eyes (like her father), I could see what a blessing she was meant to be. Once she had been weighed and checked for all the correct infant vital signs, she was handed to me, her father, to look after from now until eternity.

I started to talk to Christina, and she focused her attention on me with those sapphires eyes—no kidding! From all the wonderful chats that I had with her in Mummy's tummy, she knew the voice of her father! I was on cloud nine as I pranced up and down many halls of that London, ON hospital showing off to everyone who would notice my beautiful child, Christina Walker.

When we brought Christina home and let her get familiar with the nursery, Dad insisted that we begin to read and sing to her. I believe that Christina's love for language (or languages) combined with music is a result of the early nurturing that we consistently followed as part of her regular routine for three years. I think that our goals for Christina's future communication and comprehension skills greatly benefited her development through a simple yet effective method of classical and worship music.

But even the tiny things I tried to do in being a good and supportive father seemed to upset Gwen. Having just breastfed the child in the middle of the night, Gwen would ask me to do my share of the load—burping the baby and putting her back to sleep. After her feeding, I would hold her for a proper burp and settle her down by singing spirituals. Once the deed of the burping was done, Christina would go right back to sleep. At times it would appear to me that my involvement and touch with Christina would irritate Gwen, as she claimed that she didn't have the soothing touch to put our child back to sleep. Christina appeared to feel secure knowing that her dad's singing voice could lull her to sleep.

When Christina was one and just learning to walk, Great-grandma Violet gave her a beautiful, blue smocked dress with delicate baby embroidery all over it. Christina loved to wear this outfit and would toddle to the front door to greet her daddy. Her first word at ten months old was: "Dadda." She would thrill my heart with her excited shrieks as she came running to Daddy with her arms outstretched, ready to greet me, as she gave me wonderful hugs and kisses. Her actions filled my heart with such love and joy.

Christina was a very happy toddler, and she loved it when I would pick her up, pretend I was an airplane, and then spin her around. After Christina's first birthday, and watching Gwen as a new mother, I became concerned as I noticed a growing dependence on just the mother and child relationship.

Gwen had wanted to be able to stay home full-time for a least two years and then return to her teaching position; however, due to my employment situation, we could not afford for her to do so. Gwen decided to take some maternity time off, get acquainted with the baby's schedule, and then return to work. It did appear to me that she was resentful of this family decision.

After Gwen's family trip to Florida (which I could not attend, nor was I invited) in Christina's second year, I felt that she became quite negative toward me, and I felt emotionally destroyed. I thought it was just emotional exhaustion. The emotional environment in our home changed.

Gwen and Christina had what I believe was a closed and exclusive relationship. This closeness in their relationship continues to this day. I felt as though I were being gradually excluded from Christina's life. The bitterness and confusion grew rapidly between Gwen and me and in our communications. Feeling helpless and alone, I couldn't understand how to change the situation.

I tried rationalizing these emotions. Gwen then told me that she didn't love me anymore and asked me to leave our home. I was shocked and wounded, and my attempts to discuss our situation seemed futile.

The relationship between us no longer existed, nor did I want to be around Gwen; we were just two different people that didn't agree on anything. From an ADD/ADHD perspective, I was spinning like a top. My emotions were all over the place, and it wasn't until I was in my own, safe environment that I could access and create a strategy of "next steps." I was very focused on seeing the *Break Thru TV* project become a success and hopefully develop into a TV series. While we were in the initial stages of a separation, I became aware that Gwen thought I wouldn't be interested in having a relationship with Christina, as I was focused on my own interests and musical career.

After seven years of marriage, I was overjoyed to have a child of my own. I wanted a family. I would not back down on having a relationship with Christina. I tried to be a solid support by taking on more daily assistance with Christina's caregiving needs, but that was met with resistance. Strangely enough, I began to turn my resentment toward Christina. Once I understood what was really going on, I realized I couldn't blame my daughter. After all, she was just a little child growing up in a very dysfunctional home.

During this time, I decided that it would be best for all of us if I was just on my own and no longer living in London. Besides, the opportunity to jumpstart my broadcasting and ministry was before me. My second thought was how to maintain a relationship with my daughter outside of London when an uncooperative ex-spouse could make my new life as a separated father a living nightmare. Complicated by ADHD, this time was emotionally and unbearably stressful.

Though it wasn't immediately evident to me at the time, there was no unity in our home about my career or my musical longings or opportunities. This, combined with my struggle with ADHD, vitiated my marriage.

Any illness or physical or emotional dysfunction takes a heavy toll on both parties. Undiagnosed ADHD is riddled with misunderstanding, anger, mistrust, and hopelessness. Recent studies of ADHD spouses (who have lived with a spouse for longer than ten years) have indicated that life is not easy for the other partner. There are many ups and downs with employment issues and coping with the mood disorders. For most adults with ADHD, medication is needed, resulting in inevitable addiction. Thankfully, prescription medicine was not needed for me! We all have a breaking point and, in my opinion, I know where that breaking point occurred. The stresses in our relationship, plus the difficulty of my personal disorder, absolutely killed the marriage.

I did not know until the mid-1990s (and until I sought some professional help) how to fix the problems between us. I did know that a lot of my own frustration concerned where we were living. London was not a cosmopolitan city and did not provide solid career options. I wanted to move closer to Toronto, but Gwen did not want to move. We were at an impasse.

In my opinion, from an ADD/ADHD perspective, I felt used about my family situation and the obstacles to seeing my daughter, and even though my physical disability couldn't be seen, my emotions and mental state were in tatters. I felt I was being pushed to the edge of the cliff. My mind ran like a never-ending movie with no let-up! I needed medication to let my mind rest and my body to sleep. Constantly distraught, I would go to bed, only to wake up very early the next morning. There was a constant rehearsal of actions or reactions and negative thoughts. On top of feeling exhausted, I shed many tears. Accomplishing any task that day was out of the question. These thoughts and emotions soon developed into a dark depression.

During our three years of separation, and throughout Christina's teenage years, I did not have regular access and family time with Christina, which caused my emotional state to flare. I often felt completely emotionally barren—and very angry. Having joint custody for my daughter's emotional sake could have been the answer, but this was never agreed to.

During the first few years of our separation and later divorce, I attempted written communication. I wanted closure. Over these last twenty years, I have confessed all my own personal failures to Gwen and ultimately to Christina. My comments have never been acknowledged. A dear friend shared with me that if you have gone to the fence and admitted your mistakes, asked for forgiveness, and not received forgiveness in return, then there really is nothing more you can do. God will honour your diligence. I come to the Lord daily, wanting to be clean before Him in my heart and in my issues of forgiveness regarding Gwen.

Lurking underneath the failed marriage and my deeply emotional, sometimes chaotic and heartbroken response, was my as-yet undiagnosed condition of ADHD. There I was thinking I was a committed husband and father giving it my all. Yes, I acknowledged that I was creative and unusual—but I did not discern the pattern of behaviours that were shouting "ADHD! ADHD!"

Had I been diagnosed earlier, who knows? I'm not convinced that Gwen's and my personalities could have been happy together anyway. As a committed believer, I am deeply grieved that there has been no unity or attempt to resolve our issues on all sides. This has been Gwen's choice. The option to hold on to our painful past and differences has been her choice. Healing is the believer's birth right, if you are interested!

CHAPTER SIXTEEN
STANDING ON STAGE, JUST OUTSIDE OF THE SPOTLIGHTS

"No one can make you feel inferior without your consent," is a frequently quoted statement attributed to Eleanor Roosevelt. Jane Fonda—Hollywood actress, Christian, writer/author, and icon, (whom I greatly admire)—states her personal revelation in her book, *My Life So Far*[10], in referencing and in putting up with abusive people in her past relationships. Jane writes about these folks as they tried to bully her and make her life and actions seem inferior.

I don't know if it was the denial or shock with the change of climate in the household, but I constantly felt inferior! Once I was aware of these factors through therapy, I concluded that enough was enough! I would never again give anyone permission to make me feel inferior ... or, as from the musical *Funny Girl*, Barbra Streisand so richly continues to sing, "No one is going to rain on my parade!"

---

[10] Jane Fonda, *My Life so Far* (Toronto: Random House, 2005), 403.

Following the birth of our daughter, Christina, in 1991, the deep cracks in the foundation of our marriage began to be exposed. Our co-dependent behaviour was expressed in our "I need you to need me" approach to life. Co-dependence is so insidious that if one partner in the relationship gets healthier and not so dependent, the other partner can go to extreme lengths to sabotage that progress and growth. Co-dependence was a strong factor during our high school days, our courtship years, and all the way through to the end of our marriage.

I also learned from my therapy sessions that another destructive and oppressive force was working against us. Our union was impacted by the satanic effects of "Freemasonry" through both sides of our family lineages. Once gaining this understanding through reading, searching, and attending many seminars on Freemasonry, I saw demonic attempts to ruin healthy family relationships.

Through prayer, I sought God for help. I wanted to be free, healed, and restored. Could we have a chance to build again from the ground up? Through the Holy Spirit—and with the guidance of my counsellors—we had hope.

Sometime following the announcement of our separation, I ran into the pastor who had officiated at our wedding. In expressing his sadness over the news of our separation, he said, "Ian, of all the people that I know, you are a true believer. I know that you were raised right, in a loving Christian home. I really believed that you could have made a difference in Gwen's spiritual life."

For three years, I remained hopeful and steadfast with much intercession. Unfortunately, it became evident that a divorce was the only option. To this day, there is no eye contact or conversation with my ex-wife. Sadly, this is also the case in dealing with Christina's needs. The idea of not communicating one's feelings, seeking forgiveness, and then getting on with life was totally alien to me.

During my access weekends with young Christina, we would go to the park. We would swing together, and we would talk. She would ask me, "Why are you and Mommy so sad?"

I truly can relate to the movie *I Am Sam*, starring Sean Penn, Dakota Fanning, and Michelle Pfeiffer. This amazing story is about a mentally challenged father who passionately loves his daughter. Despite losing custody through an action of the state, Lucy is his entire world. Christina was my entire world, and she loved to be with her daddy!

The scenes in this movie brought back many unhappy memories. I felt hopeless. Despite trying to work out a reasonable child visitation plan, other people were controlling my life, and I deeply resented that! My ADHD symptoms were all over the map! I went through a devastating, emotional five years by consulting lawyers, therapists, and social workers. Trying to secure visitation rights with my daughter was a nightmare!

During these years of separation and divorce, I witnessed Gwen's constant need to be in control. My integrity was put into question by the untrue stories shared by Gwen to the court system, church pastors, or anyone else who would listen to her. My mother used to say to us siblings, "Your sins will find you out." I have chosen to walk in forgiveness; however, this is not reciprocated by Gwen.

I was hopeful that, for at least for our daughter's benefit, we could be civil to each other. This is not the case. I am trusting in God to heal this relationship in His way and His timing. Another dear friend quoted this statement to me: "The only power that we have is the power of choice!" Amen!

***

I found balance and stability as a member of the Toronto Airport Christian Fellowship (TACF, now known as Catch the Fire Ministries), my home church for the last twenty years. A few times on a Friday evening or during a Saturday afternoon conference, I would just need more of a "soaking-type" time with the Lord. This is when I would come into His presence, bringing all my emotional baggage with me.

One time I was deeply troubled and could barely stand for the worship time. I made my way back behind the stage into an open-aired area, just needing some quiet time to myself. The Holy Spirit spoke to me: "Ian, lie down and worship me, and I'll bring peace to your spirit." Knowing clearly when the Holy Spirit was speaking to me in His fatherly and caring way, I obeyed. Almost instantly I experienced a deep peace in the presence of the Lord. The next thing I knew, two hours had passed. God had lifted the burdens. All anxieties were gone! What an awesome Heavenly Daddy we serve!

I have a great circle of Christian friends and couples who loved Christina and who tried to make her feel at home and encourage interaction with their children when we would visit. Christina now claims that she doesn't remember these fun experiences or the positive interaction with these other families, combined with lots of laughter and sheer fun! I wanted her to have some positive memories of being around happy and normal Christian families, without all of the drama that was occurring in both of our lives.

Presently, Christina is in post-graduate studies, and we are rebuilding our relationship slowly. In our ongoing interactions, I can see that Christina is still hurt. I am hopeful that in the near future, and with some counselling, the past can be put to rest and we can truly walk in forgiveness.

As you can tell, these memories and events happened to me, dear reader. You may have similar scenarios in your life or family. Perhaps like me you have had some challenges as a learning disabled parent, and you don't know how to protect yourself or your rights. You are at a total loss as to how to obtain a secure and non-demeaning, non-bullying, or destructive environment in which to exercise your legal child access arrangements. God willing, after the separation or divorce, you can develop parental and healthy relationships with your children.

In retrospect, if I had been granted joint custody, I don't know how my present relationship with Christina would be different for us both today. From living through such a nightmare experience, I have become a very strong advocate and believer in court protection to secure fathers' rights. Joint custody could have worked much better for me and Christina. Recently, Canadian laws have changed, and independent single mothers cannot just get custody on their own without the father's involvement.

What concerns me now are the emotional scars that Gwen and I have both inflicted on our daughter's future relationships and her perception of men. I take these issues before the Lord weekly. Presently, as I grow deeper with the Heavenly Father, I'm learning how to forgive myself and others.

Jesus will indeed be our advocate. I no longer need to defend myself from the past.

In my initial counselling sessions post-separation, I learned that I was living in a one-sided, abusive, and bullying relationship. Just about everything during this period had to be "Gwen's way" to keep the peace. She demeaned me through the process of creating ongoing and artistic projects. All this negative "banter" from her literally fueled my ADHD and eroded my self-esteem. Had I not received overwhelming support from my family and the dear, close friends that stood beside me, I may not have been able to be here today to share my story with you.

Celebrating with Mom, Dad, and Elaine at my McMaster University Convocation in June 2009. (Walker Family Photo Collection)

TRANSITION, TRANSFORMATION, AND TRANSCENDENCE

Lest I give the impression that I am stuck in a cycle of pain and unforgiveness, let me tell you the joy of my transitions, transformation, and my discovery of transcendence. In a way, one could say I have moved on with my life. But that is too simple. It is also misleading. With as much inner turmoil and emotional injury that I have endured, there is no such thing as simply moving on.

Remember when I mentioned God moments? It's impossible to list and expound on the impact of those God moments. When connected, they made a God chain of healing.

Transition: watch for the Change. In addition to God's faithful and patient guidance and healing, I have rejoiced in the wonderful loving affection and support of others. I have celebrated their ongoing belief in me. I found the strength to refocus.

These are the people who continuously encourage me. Thus, I have achieved many of the goals and projects that I wanted to accomplish before I reached the age of fifty! With these accomplishments have come professional and personal recognition. Validation came through obtaining varied educational degrees and community awards.

Transformation: watch God work. Christina was jaundiced toward me by her mother and in any way that I tried to improve myself or by seeking the university or graduate-level education that I needed. Thus, when these university or college convocations took place, Christina wasn't allowed to attend or support me as my family and close friends did. Tale-bearing and back biting are indeed sins, and Gwen is responsible for her words and actions; however, my Father God is so protective of my heart that His participation "through it all" has proven to be more than sufficient.

Receiving the MAPS-Centennial Award, alongside both McMaster University presidents (the incoming Dr. Patrick Deane and the outgoing late Dr. Peter George) in November 2010 (ECG Photo Collection)

Transcendence: let God lift you above it. This personal family turmoil was the darkest walk of "the valley of my soul" that I had ever had to walk through in my life. Only God could have walked alongside of me, taken me firmly by the hand, and lifted me out of this very painful pit by giving me strength to embark on a healing journey.

The negative attempts to prevent reconciliation continue to this day; however, I have learned to continually give these deep emotional hurts to the Lord. I know that Jesus and His loving and powerful Spirit move rapidly on my behalf when I choose the way of His transcendence.

Looking back, I can see the progression. From childhood I was teased, taunted, terrorized, talked about, troubled, trampled on, and traumatized. Whew! But somehow, in the middle of it all and by the grace of God, I was also tenacious. I still had faith for a transition in my life. I held out for a transformation I knew only God could orchestrate. As a result, I have experienced what it's like to be a transcendent child of God. But just like Elijah's servant, I was sent time and again to look for a sign of God's presence and help. The servant saw a cloud no bigger than the size of a man's hand in the sky. It was about to rain. Yes, indeed, God was up to something. It was a sign of change.

Like anyone else, I spent many sleepless nights pondering questions concerning family, faith, and future. Except for the Lord and a few close friends and family, I had no one to whom I could express my true, deep anguish of the soul. But that was in the years BE—before Elaine.

My DNA, birthright, and destiny were formed and refined through these initial experiences for my development in the Christian arts. Only Jesus understands the true intentions in my heart when, on my knees, weeping, I asked Him to come and heal my damaged emotions and the actual wrenching physical pain of being separated from my daughter.

God would provide His spirit and bring His peace through the solace of listening to praise and worship music. And it worked! The music ministered deep within my aching soul. This touch of the supernatural is when I started to understand God's purpose and plan for my life. I could identify with Joseph in the Old Testament. After spending time living in the pit, my life was about to take an upward turn.

There would be joy and another wonderful woman to love me like no one person has loved me before—God's generous gift, "my precious Elaine!" Our relationship blossomed year by year through a fun courtship and now a marriage for a lifetime. Let me take you back to the beginning of the transcendence out of the pit.

In 1995, I was living with my parents (for just one year and half) post my three year separation from Gwen. I was so desperate for God that I would spend my devotion times with the Lord in the early mornings. One morning I was on my knees, weeping before the Lord, talking to Him about my brokenness, and wanting restoration. In my mind's eye, I could see Jesus right there with me, and I talked to Him about my sorrow. Opening my eyes, all I could see around me were His legs and His feet. He was standing there with me while I poured out my heart. That intimate moment with Jesus gave me the needed strength to endure the remaining months until I would be divorced.

My story is much like the story of Joseph—a period of living in prison-like torment until God reveals the next part of the journey and clarifies one's testimony. It has been said before that "there has to be a test before there can be a testimony." Because of this destructive period in my personal life, I would gain total freedom in other areas of my Christian walk and be able to minister to others who were hurting in much the same way. But walking this faith walk and following through with "walking the talk" are a testimony that comes at a great cost!

The power of the resurrected Christ is right here. As you call out Jesus' name, you gain an intimate and personal relationship with Him! That part is absolutely free for the asking. Jesus paid the entire cost for you to have all your sins completely washed away. At that point, you stand blameless and pure, totally forgiven. But that's only the beginning. As you begin your faith walk, you will discover that being used of Him, sent by Him, and being effective for Him are costly.

His anointing comes at great cost! The more I surrendered the failures, the hopeless situations, the deep cuts and wounds to Jesus, the deeper I could feel His redeeming love. His magnificent love flowed over my head, my spirit, and my soul, healing and touching my wounds, and they began to heal. Finally, I could hear my soul singing again … singing that Jesus truly loves and is so passionate for me! I have listened to many sincere testimonies of others whose hearts have also been broken. I've heard traumatic stories and accounts of negative relationship situations very similar to mine.

Many turn to medication. No doubt about it, medication can help. Getting expert pharmacological assistance makes perfect sense, especially in the beginning stages of coping with the initial shock and trauma of a serious physical and emotional break-up. I suggest that should you need medication for a season, based on your doctor's recommendation, take it as a gift from God. Based on my personal experience, I know that it is only through God's grace and His loving guidance that one can truly begin the process of restoration—eventually even without the aid of medication.

Elaine and I both see much fruit in our ministry as we minister to others who are currently in similar painful marital or other agonizing situations, separated from their own children. And this is the advice that we offer to them.

Believe in yourself. Take small steps and let God heal you, brain cell by brain cell, and wounded limb by limb. In His expert and tender care, you will be on the road to recovery … if, that is, you will begin to listen to God's small voice speaking to you in this time of brokenness. Hear and obey Him and, bit by bit, the healing will begin. God will speak to you and answer you—but be patient! The process can be slow.

Before you a take another giant step, remember that your spirit and soul have been crushed, and you want to make sure that you are clearly hearing from God. My advice is to take small steps. Surround yourself with caring and loving people who believe in you. Ask those whom you can trust to listen to your sorrows and to comfort you when you need to get this poison of past hurts and deep pains out of your spirit. Give them permission to speak correction when necessary. And ask them to keep your confidences. Ask them to pray with and for you. Through the extended body of Christ, let the healing of the Holy Spirit surround you with His tender blanket of peace. Accept His assurance that you are safe and that He will heal all your personal damage. Then trust Him to perform it in His perfect time.

If you have not been released by a person who has sinned against you, set the situation before God and ask Him to help you make sure that your heart is clean. Pray for His instruction for the next steps toward peace of mind and in leaving the past behind.

Together, Elaine and I have prayed over this book and for those readers who are currently in marital trouble or similarly separated from their own children due to some ADD/ADHD emotional circumstances. Far too many have felt and understand this pain. Our hope is to foster your healing. Our purpose is to lead you to Christ.

CHAPTER SEVENTEEN
ELAINE—ENTER STAGE LEFT
By W. Ian and Elaine Walker

In May of 1995, Elaine was re-introduced to me. Later she would become my girlfriend, my sweetheart, and my life partner!

Our story began in 1978 at a Christian roller skating event in Hamilton when Elaine's close friend, Melanie, introduced us to each other. Melanie was then dating a family friend, Victor. As divine coincidence would have it, Victor's dad worked with Elaine's dad in the jewellery business. When Elaine and I first met we were cordial, and our initial encounter lasted only a few brief minutes. We didn't re-connect until eighteen years later. Another divine coincidence occurred when Elaine and I shared mutual friends from Crossfire Assembly.

The home of Crossfire Assembly of Hamilton was the former Tivoli Theatre, and it was one of my favourite movie theatres when I was in my teens. Built in 1912, the structure resembled a vaudevillian theatre of its day. It was resplendent with its arched ceilings and lavish Edwardian architecture. In the 1970s, this theatre was refitted with state-of-the-art Dolby sound. I remember attending and watching the first of the two *Star Wars* films there. By the mid-90s, the theatre was owned by Sam Sniderman (Sam the Record Man, Canadian chain), and the building had been empty for several years.

Crossfire's board of directors enquired about the building, and they could negotiate a lease from Mr. Sniderman for only $1.00 per year. The church was responsible for all the utilities plus needed repairs to this grand old building. This venue was Crossfire Assembly's home for about five years and they served as host to many great speakers, Christian musicians, dancers, preachers, and awesome Holy Ghost conventions.

Sadly, in 2003, costly repairs were required on the roof, and this grand old dame of the entertainment and movie circuit collapsed. The subsequent natural decaying of the building left some serious structural core problems, and eventually its historic "Versace-mirrored entrance" had to be torn down. The news that this dwelling place and former theatre were no longer in existence truly broke my heart.

I have often reflected on these amazing moments and times of the Holy Spirit's presence at Crossfire Assembly. On November 5, 1857, a New York newspaper carried a story of a revival in Hamilton, Ontario, Canada. It was reported that three hundred to four hundred people were converted in a few days. This spiritual dusting of the 1800s was completely transformed when revival hit Hamilton, Ontario in the mid-1990s. That's when internationally known and respected prophet, the late Jill Austin of Master Potter Ministries, came to Hamilton. She added even more gold to the spiritual climate of the city. Jill and other authentic prophets of God have declared that Hamilton, Ontario will see another such revival in the city in the coming years. I can't wait to see these prophetic words and events happen in my hometown again!

Jill ministered at our church for about three days. During that visit, she received a credible word of the Lord for me. As she spoke the prophetic words over me, the fire of God was indeed released within me. Involuntarily, I shook and fell under the power of God. Slowly, getting back on my feet, I could feel and see the fire of God all around me. Jill received the following prophetic words and said them over me:

> "You have been called forth as a mighty man of God who will do great things for the arts—restoring the arts to my real intention. You have been tested and it has been a time to purify you of all of the wood, hay, and stubble elements of your life so that these giftings and callings that I have placed within you, since birth, may come to the surface and be demonstrated to this current and next generation. You have a great sensitivity to My Holy Spirit, and you know, hear, and obey His voice. I am calling you forth as a General and as a keeper of my pure, "godly" way that the Christian arts will be presented in the future. You will create, write, and produce many productions, and in the future, your work will have My stamp of excellence upon it."

I had no real understanding of the power of those prophetic words until the 2000s. Just as a steer is branded to identify its owner, those prophetic words are now branded within my heart. Jill Austin's transforming word was yet another confirmation that I did hear from God in stepping out in faith to initially produce *Break Thru TV*. In times of doubt or frustration, just reading those prophetic words out loud quickens my spirit. I feel God's anointing over these words.

In preparing for the publication of this book, I was in touch with Jill's office, seeking permission to use this prophetic word in print. Jill was thrilled by my testimony and was looking forward to meeting me again at a future conference. In January 2009, I heard the very sad news that Jill Austin had passed away and is now dancing with the Lord. Our meeting and reunion will have to wait until the family of believers are together again in Heaven.

Previously, in the mid-1990s I was glad to be a part of Crossfire Assembly. Here I was slowly healing from my wounds. The members of our church fellowship had ministered to many street persons across the city and then continued to be very active in evangelical meetings and positively impacting the spiritual climate of the city. As the Tivoli Theatre was being cleaned up and restored again within the local community, I too was being restored after my separation and my pending divorce. The church's wonderful Christian counselling team assisted me greatly. Once again, bit by bit, the Holy Spirit was redeeming me, restoring my soul, and re-establishing me as a confident man. He was preparing me for a new relationship with Elaine.

Born with cerebral palsy in September of 1958, Elaine Ruth Midori Kawai was born prematurely, weighing only two pounds seven ounces. The use of forceps was required for the doctors to bring the baby to safety, which resulted in her injury and disability. With the use of braces on her legs, she began to walk at the age of five. Elaine endured four surgeries to walk and had a difficult childhood. Born into a Japanese Canadian family, she has two older brothers and one younger. Elaine and her brothers were raised in the Buddhist religion. Elaine tells her own experiences and story here:

> "Growing up, I faced many challenges, but that never stopped me from getting where I wanted to go. Eventually, my tenacity would pay off and I would gain victory. I was limited to what I could do physically, except during my fourth-grade gym class at school. I would play deck tennis in the school gym. The goal of the game is to throw the ring into the opponent's court. The opponent tries to catch it before it falls and immediately throws it back from the same position where it was caught. A point is scored when the server manages to land a quoit (a rubber donut-shaped ring) on the opponent's side of the court.
>
> "I didn't use a crutch and moved in rotation with the rest of my teammates. When it came my time to serve, I could throw that ring just like the next person. In Grade Five, I played on a lunch hour baseball team. I would get up to bat and a runner would be there to run the bases after I hit the ball. I played outfield position. I never caught the ball much out there, but it felt good.

I was participating in a sport and, as a result, my self-image grew stronger.

"Later in my high school years, I joined a swimming team for the disabled. There were eight members on my swim team. One of the team had missing limbs at birth, some had cerebral palsy, and one team member was partially blind and had difficulty walking. We would train a few days a week at two local pools. The training was grueling to say the least. We trained long and hard. The first year I trained in the breast stroke, as I did not have much use of my legs for kicking. Most of my movement in the water came from the strength in my arms, stemming from the use of crutches. I competed in the regional games to qualify for the Ontario Games for the Physically Disabled. In 1977, I won the bronze medal for the breast stroke. The very next year, I won the gold medal for the twenty-five-metre front crawl.

"Several years later, I returned to school to develop new skills. Sponsored by the Ontario March of Dimes, I attended Mohawk College and earned my certificate in the Micro Computer Business Applications Program. Eight computer courses were offered. Based on the prerequisite testing and an interview, I was accepted into the program—free of charge! Completing a year of study, I graduated from the program and was subsequently offered a job in an administrative position with the federal government of Canada. Just recently, I celebrated twenty years working for the government. I do give all the glory to the Lord for His provision in my life."

Elaine would frequently attend Crossfire Assembly as a visitor, and she would notice me and inquire, "Who is this tall, broken man who always wears a suit to church and is at the altar weeping?"

I would indeed be kneeling at the altar, weeping and asking God, "Lord, am I in your will right now? By being alone, out here in the wilderness?" Oh, how I wanted God to heal my heart and my mind from all the pain.

A mutual friend, Neil, had mentioned my name to Elaine several times. One evening Elaine invited us both over to her place to get better acquainted. In her memory bank, there was something uncanny. She felt that she had made a connection with me in the past, but I couldn't remember our first meeting. One evening, Neil and I were going to a church community event, but first we stopped off at Elaine's. After being invited in, she and I both stared at each other. Where was it? We were both trying to remember where it was that we had met. Finally, Elaine broke the ice. "Do you remember, or do you know, my good friend, Melanie?" Instantly we remembered our first encounter.

From that moment and as much as I would let her into my life, we became friends. I was very hesitant to get into any relationship at that stage of my life. I was not yet divorced from Gwen, and I believed in my heart that there was still hope. For two and a half years I prayed, asking my close family and friends to pray in agreement with me. In my heart, I didn't believe in divorce, especially for Christians.

Elaine felt that her mission in my life was to be my friend and to be an intercessor. Only after God revealed to us that we should stop praying for the former relationship did our friendship connection begin to develop into a new courtship. We were learning to be obedient to God as the Holy Spirit would lead us. Early in December of 1995, I received my preliminary divorce papers.

What would this new single status mean for me? At the age of thirty-six, I didn't know how to function as a newly single man. This feeling of singleness was very foreign to me. My natural self repeatedly screamed at me, "What are you doing? You have been severely burned by another female relationship, yet your divorce isn't even settled. Wake up! You're not ready for this!" Yet in special moments with Elaine, my heart was turning toward her and her many wonderful, godly, and childlike qualities. Elaine is truly a spiritually strong warrior and intercessor.

Elaine and I were good friends going into our relationship. I would come to her home and she would cook for me or make special foods and desserts. We felt blessed just to hang out or watch movies together. Often, we would pray and intercede for mutual friends.

God gave me a wakeup call as He showed me that there was to be a season of mourning. There was also a period of restoration of my calling as a worshipper and artist. This awareness was life-giving. It was the beginning of walking in freedom. I was going forth with my family's biblical foundations intact and secure. I was called to be a carrier of the anointing of God. I was being reprogrammed as a man of God.

As my counselling and healing sessions continued, I would, in time, be able to use all the giftings that were placed within me as an artist—a baritone soloist, a worship leader, and in the 2000s, the Artist Director and Conductor for the Youth Choir for the Nations. These talents and skills had laid dormant for many years; however, in the 2000s, God opened the desires of my heart. At six months into my new relationship with Elaine, I could sense God's love and His oil of grace falling all over me. As the Psalmist says, oil will be anointed from the top of my head to the bottoms of my feet (Psalm 133:2, paraphrase).

It's not surprising that I also needed to address some personal issues between me and my parents and siblings. Childhood fears and emotional traumas had led me to behave in such a wounded manner. I needed to confront my parents in love when they had told me that my way of thinking was wrong. Later, through ADHD counselling, I learned that I was entitled to think and process the way I did, and it was not wrong! It simply was my way. No one has the right to question your individual way of thinking by stating that your way is wrong!

Many times I had asked my parents' forgiveness for the times I had hurt them. I had repented to them for those times when I had broken down communications and shattered their trust. After this time of open dialogue and forgiveness between my parents and me, the forgiveness began to flow between all family members. God's blessings opened a new and excellent relationship with my parents and my siblings. Forgiveness was the key!

I began to see a glimmer of hope, which included building a stable and loving relationship with Elaine. We would become engaged in 1996, and with these plans underway, my family welcomed Elaine with open arms. She brought much healing and laughter. With pre-marital counselling, we were sure our relationship could become a happy marriage.

All my family and close friends could see the smile on my face and that all was well in Ian's world. Elaine's redeeming grace was a critical factor in our new, blossoming relationship with Christina as we entered the initial stages of becoming a blended family. The spring in my step returned, and my sense of humour came back in full force. Everyone could sense Elaine's genuine spirit and her truthfulness, and that her Christian faith walk was authentic. Together we are not only both survivors, but thrivers in overcoming our disabilities issues. We can see God blessing us as a couple with aspirations in ministry.

Elaine and I had developed some amazing and loyal Christian friends. Byron Humphrey is a retired educator who had taught special needs children, and he is a great friend and proofreader and editor of my prose. One of those most precious couples that we are still in constant communication with is the Jones family (Jill was our Matron of Honour and Gary was one of our groomsman at our wedding) and the late Craig Sproats and Marie Patenaude. We can't forget our loving friends, Cheryl and Leon Sebrins, with whom we share many interests in music, dance, and intercession for Canada.

Craig Sproats and I were very close, best friends. We were like the biblical relationship of Jonathon and David. Craig was a tremendous support to both Elaine and me. He helped me throughout my many activities as an artist/writer and became my first board member when we formed the Youth Choir for the Nations choral ensemble. He left this earth too early, in his late fifties, in 2009. He was an older brother figure to me when I needed his advice. I miss Craig, his laughter, and our fun times together. Craig blessed my life with his friendship for over fifteen years.

OBTAINING PARENTAL CONSENT FOR MARRIAGE TO ELAINE

In November 1996, Elaine and I decided that we wanted to get married and that we needed to ask her parents' permission. We both knew that Christina was at peace with our decision. I had returned to McMaster University to finish up two years of credits that I needed to complete for my BA. Here I was, the second time, about to ask a father for his daughter's hand in marriage. I am very old-fashioned, and I am so glad that I got his blessing.

Showing this level of respect to my father-in-law-to-be opened many wonderful doors of communication between Elaine's parents, Alice and Frank, and myself. I couldn't have asked for better in-laws! Frank was a passionate sportsman who passed away in January 2017, just short of his ninety-third birthday. We all miss him and remember favourite sports to watch on TV—golf, baseball, hockey, and football. He was the best father-in-law to me, and now being in the family some twenty years later, he was my best buddy to talk over all of life's issues and problems. Frank delayed his retirement as a jeweller until he was eighty-eight years young.

I need to thank the Toronto Blue Jays baseball team for winning an important game on the day we approached Elaine's parents for her hand in marriage. (Frank was a huge Blue Jays baseball fan.) That win made my life so much easier, as Frank was in a great mood when I asked him for permission to marry Elaine. Finally, when the house was quiet post-game and it was down to just the four of us, I asked the question to Frank. Both Frank and Alice extended their approval and blessing to marry their daughter. Next item on the agenda would be to set the date for our wedding.

We went to Frank's jewellery store to pick out our rings and for Elaine to show me a few of her choices of an engagement ring. My parents were happy for me and they again welcomed Elaine as their future daughter-in-law into the family. When Elaine's ring was ready, I picked it up, but I waited until Christina was with us again. I wanted her to witness how a man should propose to a woman. I got down on one knee in front of Christina and Elaine and then asked Elaine if she would marry me. Truly it was a family affair! Elaine responded "yes," and I placed the ring on her finger. Elaine tells how she planned to purchase her wedding dress.

"Now that I was engaged, I was pushing forward on the wedding plans. Although it was raining that day, I decided to take the bus and go downtown in Hamilton to look at wedding dresses. There were at least three wedding boutiques on our main street. As the bus came to my desired stop, I got off and headed toward the first shop. I walked in and told the saleslady what I was looking for. We proceeded to look for the perfect dress. Nothing. So I proceeded to the next two shops and did the same. Still nothing.

The very idea of looking for a wedding dress made me so excited that I was oblivious to anything else around me. When I left the third store, the wind and the rain had picked up. The wind gusts were so strong that I could not even walk. I had to grab onto actual sides of the buildings as I attempted to stand up and get back to the bus stop for my ride home. It was absolute torture! I was scared for my life battling those high winds and torrential downpours.

The strong wind blew against me until I felt I could not move or breathe. Finally, I made it back to the bus stop just in time to catch my bus and make it back home safe and sound. But I realized I was battling more than the wind and the rain. Something was not right.

If this was God directing me to look at a wedding dress, where was His peace? I didn't sense His peace at all that morning. In fact, I experienced just the opposite. Bound and determined to get downtown, I was going to look at those dresses no matter what! My determination turned to stubbornness, and I had been in strife the whole morning. As a result, I had lost God's peace. Something was off, and it was not in His timing."

As we began to make wedding plans for the spring of 1997, something was not right. Everything that we tried to do in booking the hall, arranging for the invitations and flowers, and even in asking the right bridesmaids to be a support for Elaine was just not working out. It was extremely frustrating!

The late Catherine Visseau felt that she had a word from the Lord on the situation. Hesitant and wanting to be sure, she told God that if I called her that very evening, she would tell me what she sensed the Lord was saying. Otherwise, she wouldn't give that prophetic word to me. I did call Catherine that night, and I shared with her that our plans were just not going so well. Little did I realize my remarks would free Catherine to speak but would also require some pain and a lengthy season of waiting for Elaine and me. Catherine said: "Everything is not right. Do you remember the passage in the Bible about the preparation for the wedding banquet? I sense that everything is not prepared yet. If you two will wait a bit, maybe for a year or so, God will supply everything that you need."

That was a very hard word for a young, disabled woman who had waited twenty-three years for the man of God's choosing to come into her life, only now to be told to wait a little bit longer. We were at a weekend Christian conference when we received, processed, and obtained confirmation of this prophetic word. We then committed this word back to the Lord and to the ministerial leadership around us, who covered us in prayer.

Through our tears, we knew this delay was right, so we decided that we would wait. Of all the prophetic words that we have received over the years of our courtship to marriage, this word was the hardest, but it was also 100 per cent accurate!

God indeed blessed us for our obedience, and when the time was right for all the preparations, we witnessed the most awesome connections and events happen for our wedding on June 26, 1999. We are now in our almost third decade of commitment in a wonderful relationship together. We continue to have great moments of pure laughter, totally enjoying each other's company.

Combined with our walk with the Lord, being with Elaine has provided much stability, trust, commitment, companionship, and the healing presence of the Lord. Her persona in my life gives me breathing room and has helped me handle all the excess drama that took place during those transition years being a single dad. From that cordial coincidence on a roller-skating rink many years ago, to a stable marriage based on our shared relationship and following together with our calling, I must say that chance meeting led to a "God encounter" for us both that will last forever into eternity.

CHAPTER EIGHTEEN
GROWTH SPURTS AND LEARNING CURVES

Elaine and I became loving friends. Our relationship developed into a three-year courtship. We wanted everything to be right and blessed by God's favour. Have you ever noticed that God's order means each part of the puzzle will be arranged in a timely manner? Sometimes prayers are not being answered consecutively, but simultaneously. My prayer concerns were being answered by my loving Heavenly Father.

My major concern was Christina. I wanted her to be comfortable with Elaine and with becoming a blended family. I wanted to make sure that Christina was as ready as possible to have a step-mother and a new family within the Kawai family. I knew that there was a solid friendship between Christina and Elaine.

In the mid-1990s, I also needed to rediscover who William Ian Walker really was. So many of my dreams and plans were dashed. Relationships had suffered, and at the time I just didn't know who I was or what God had really called me to do. As the butterfly in a cocoon, I had not fully developed enough strength to break out and fly. Many aspects of my ADHD symptoms still needed attention. Approaching my forties, my short-term memory loss (which is a common ADHD symptom) was a major factor. Considering the circumstances and the emotional trauma that I had endured from 1993–95, my father invited me to come home. I was in a safe place where I could recuperate. I will never forget his words. With tears in his eyes, he said, "Ian, come home. We love you. Your mother and I need to know that you are alright. You need time to put your life back together. What is it you love to do? You love to sing! So Ian, sing—and sing for the glory of God!"

Those words have meant so much to me. Dad loved me enough to open his heart and reveal his emotions. In all the years between us, he had never expressed his love so openly. Reflecting on the challenging times in my life, I now can see the Father heart of God in the same way, welcoming me home for healing and restoration.

With my father's blessing, I lived at my parents' home for the year and a half. With my mother and me having similar personalities and being under the same roof, mother's blood pressure would sometimes go sky-high. I knew that once I was healed, I would be ready to be independent. I would then get on with completing my university education. I have always been a planner, and when things don't go my way, I like to create. My wise response to keeping sane was to construct ongoing plans.

My long-term goal was to return to university and complete my BA in either music or drama. I had about half of the courses required to complete a drama degree at McMaster University in Hamilton, Ontario. I could also transfer my six credits from the Boston University Tanglewood Institute.

Part of me wanted to finish my courses and degree in music; however, I had reservations. When I considered all the necessary rehearsals, music history, theory courses, and the additional research papers demanding many hours of extra work, I had second thoughts. The lyrics from the song in *Oliver* kept ringing in my mind: "I think I better think it out again!" Realistically, this workload would be just too heavy for me. I wouldn't return to university until the fall of 1996.

USING MY PR AND MARKETING SKILLS FOR THE GYMNASTICS CHALLENGE

God was answering and leading. I was eager to get back to work. At the time, I held two contract positions—one in special events and one in fundraising. These events led me toward a career as an arts and development consultant.

In March 1995, I was hired through a grant to be Director of Marketing and Events for the Subway World Gymnastics Challenge held in Hamilton's Copps Coliseum. This employment was my first time working in an international marketing and sports venue with the American title sponsor, Subway Inc. My job involved working in marketing and special events—two areas of promotion that I enjoyed. We reported to a board of directors from Gymnastics Ontario in Toronto. In this position, I developed many skills needed to work within the media.

Partnered with an excellent writer, it was our job to identify many of the media buys and designate where we would place our radio ads. One idea came to me while watching television (seeing a scrolled ad come across the screen about a current event). I thought we could use this same technique for our Subway event by placing our ticket information on a scrolled television ad. I talked this idea over with our Subway ad agency rep, and he supported the concept. This ad generated about half of all ticket sales. From our research, we found out that many ticket-buyers would make up their minds to attend this event from viewing our television scroll ad.

Traditionally, many new business ventures hold a ribbon cutting ceremony. We did something very different. Because of the involvement of Subway Inc., and to promote our press conferences, I thought we should have two sandwiches as a "ribbon cutting" event—one in Toronto and another in Hamilton. My idea was implemented and proved to be very successful. All who attended the sandwich cutting ceremonies readily devoured the tasty sandwiches.

I was hired in March of 1995, and the event was scheduled to take place that November at Copps Coliseum, Hamilton. As director, I also sat in a volunteer capacity on the Board of Directors. From that vantage point, I observed how others would "wheel and deal." As I had worked for three different printing companies, I was able to use all my expertise. There were logos to design, stationery to choose, and ad copy to be written. Then there was the choosing of the gymnastics professionals who would appear on the poster. By a fluke, the gymnastic pros that we chose won the competition.

As part of the promotional campaign for the event, the board created a province-wide promotion. All the Subway stores would be involved in a contest to offer tickets to Atlanta's Olympic Gymnastics games in 2006. My printing agency contact and I designed the copy. Catherine Visseau, Elaine, and a few other friends were recruited to volunteer their services to hand count and sort over 50,000 ballots. For my friends' efforts, Subway would step up and supply all the great food we would need to replenish our energies.

As a close friend, Catherine gave me such positive love and support and advice. I told Catherine that she was my older and wiser sister in Christ, who was also a passionate worship leader and singer. Catherine gave me the best compliment on the opening day of the gymnastics' challenge. Seated in the VIP section along with Elaine, she said, "Wow, Ian, I can see God's and your handprint all over this project, and His level of excellence is all over you. God has big plans for your future!" I was overwhelmed by her statement but knew enough just to hand it all back to God with thanksgiving.

LOSS—LOSING GOOD FRIENDS AND FAMILY MEMBERS

Catherine Visseau was my dear and close friend for almost twenty years. Following five years of difficult health issues, she passed away. With the death of Craig Sprouts, I had lost two very dear friends only a year apart. This tough time of mourning was compounded by my mother's death in 2010 and then my father's death in 2012. I was growing up. As painful as grief can be, I was also learning how to stand on my own with God's support.

From 1996 to 1999, I was in full-time studies at McMaster University. I was prevented from seeing Christina during the Christmas Holidays of 1998. The emotional anxiety of exams for any special needs student is nearly inexplicable. Adding to this pressure, I had personal frustrations on the home front, and I was so distraught; however, God was working! I could have easily lost my second academic year in the very first term. Through His provision, I had a solid and loving relationship with Elaine. Her amazing support helped keep my sanity. I also had family and close friends within my circle of influence to keep me balanced. At that time, one tremendous friend who listened was Dr. Carol Wood, now retired from McMaster's Chaplaincy Centre. Carol provided wonderful counsel and support. I would have regular counselling sessions with Carol while I was at McMaster to just vent and try to understand what was actually going on within our family. We would talk about my "emotional capacity and my stress levels," especially from an ADHD perspective. We would then pray and ask God to bring peace to both parties, and that Christina would be protected and know that she was loved by both parents, living in separate homes.

I share these sad events to explain that a person with a disability doesn't simply cope with the ups and downs of life. ADHD people must overcompensate for all the emotional time bombs going off and all around you. At times there is nothing that can be done about it. These cruel events did lead to thoughts of suicide in hope of ending all the pain. Thankfully, my strong faith in God, and the loving support of my family, pulled me through!

I also learned from my counsellors that others were jealous of my talents. Perhaps it was my drive or energy to accomplish many goals. Who knows? Following my official diagnosis and therapy, I felt like a well-tuned Mercedes sports car. Somehow naming the problem (the truth will set you free) infused me with a new energetic spirit. I was eager to explore and tackle life! The results of the diagnostic tests determining my actual ADHD status brought many answers to the what if's I had struggled with for years. Working with professionals, I experienced a new sense of freedom. This knowledge was the beginning of Zoë understanding about me and who I really was. With this new understanding, I would soon begin to heal and then soar.

Medication did help for a season; however, the side effects were not helpful at all. I was in the public eye through sales, public relations, and marketing, as well as being on the stage. As prescribed by my doctor, I was trying two well-known antidepressant drugs. Both of these drugs caused my hands to sweat excessively. The healing process began with forgiving those who hurt me. In my counselling sessions, I confronted issues that ran from childhood to adulthood. I was learning to love me! I could just come alone to the Lord and have my devotion, worship, and intimacy with Him.

What I didn't realise until recently was that having a learning disability opens doors to feelings of guilt and shame. From reading *Deadly Emotions* by well-known Dr. Don Colbert, I now understand what damaged emotions can do to a person that suffers from ailments, and that they can later lead to depression. Dr. Colbert writes:

> Our main reason to be concerned with guilt and shame ... is this: these two states are commonly associated with major depression. Situational depression is usually the result of a major loss, in a person's life—it may be a spouse, a child, a marriage, a job, the home, or some other major loss. Guilt and shame are both rooted in what should not have occurred as much as in what did occur. Guilt is a state of having done something wrong or having committed an offense, legal or ethical. Guilt is a painful feeling of self-reproach for having done something that we recognize as being immoral, wrong, a crime, or sin. Shame generally arises from what another person has done, something the society widely recognizes as immoral, wrong, a crime, or sin—shame is the reflection on to the victim of an abuser's bad behaviour.
>
> Guilt and shame evoke different responses in us. Shame tends to create feelings of deep sorrow and sadness, as well as the lack of self-worth. Guilt produces a certain amount of danger because we feel trapped at being caught or it having fallen victim to our owned weakness. In both the emotions, however, a feeling of being worthless, hopeless, or helpless may result.
>
> These feelings, in turn, can lead to depression, anger, anxiety, another way of other toxic emotions that stimulate a stress response.

Many people link shame to painful memories of past rejection, which produces feelings of helplessness and hopelessness, or of extremely low self-value. These feelings result in depression in some, but in others they may lead to anger, resentment, or rage. Both guilt and shame create an endless circle of negative thinking. These emotions never lead to emotional freedom, strength, or health—either emotionally or physically.[11]

***

During the fall of 1998 and into the spring of 1999, I had a "once in a lifetime" opportunity to receive a great lead role in McMaster Musical Theatre's production of *Cabaret*. I was cast as "Herr Schultz, the German Jew" who owned and operated a fruit store in Berlin. Once again, I was in a role that I love! I got to use all my training and pronunciation of the German language in singing some fun yet campy duets, such as the "Pineapple Song" and "Married."

In the New Year of 1999, my bi-monthly access weekends with Christina resumed. She was seven years old and already a very good reader. Christina would help me learn my lines for this musical and the solo piece, "Meeskite." While travelling back and forth from London to Hamilton, Ontario, we would sing the song, and Christina had memorized it. That was a very special father-daughter time between us.

Around this same time, I heard the story of how Israeli olives are made into oil. When olives are freshly picked, they are placed in wagons. The olives are crushed and then pressed at a precise pressure. The fragrance of the new oil is something to smell and to experience. This fragrance and its quality only comes from being under pressure. God was doing the same refining within me. I began to sense God's deep inner cleansing. I could sense His pure, fragrant oil pouring into my soul and spirit. I watched my transformation as the old man thinking was being replaced and changed into the new man.

[11] Don Colbert, M.D., *Deadly Emotions* (Nashville: Thomas Nelson Publishers, 2003), 84–85.

"Now We Are One in You" (duet)

Elaine (Kawai) Walker and W. Ian Walker

(FEMALE)

You came into my life to take away the pain,
Deep hurts and sadness, my hopes unfilled;
I give to you my life, to honour and cherish
you,
Now and forever and forevermore.

(MALE)

You came into my life to take away the pain;
My Heart was shattered, your kindness dried
all the rain.
I pledge to you my love, my worldly goods,
my all,
Now as husband and wife, together, for the
rest of our lives,
Now and forever and forevermore.

(DUET)

Now we're together, we pledge our love and
lives to you,
Willing and ready, to obey our Master's call;
"Wither Thou Goest" we will go,
We are your servants, Lord,
Now and forevermore, Lord Jesus,
Now we are One in You!

CHAPTER NINETEEN
BECOMING ONE
By W. Ian and Elaine Walker

In writing this chapter, we decided to write from both the bride's and groom's perspectives. The production of the music and the musicians that we used in our wedding ceremony was a healing balm for my ADHD issues. When I am focused on a project large or small, and I achieve my own personal goals, my self-esteem improves greatly. We both are still in awe of how God restored two disabled persons into one anointed couple.

In the spring of 1999, everything was nearly ready. One of our dearest and oldest friends, Pastor Dennis Weidrick, had told us that when it was God's time for us to be married, it would be an imprint to the faithfulness of our God. His finest wine would be uncorked and His blessings would be on everything.

"You will have no immediate needs for finances or have any emotional needs for this wedding," he said. "You two have been faithful to God's call on your lives; you have blessed many people, and everything that you will want or desire for this event will be provided."

These words became reality! This prophetic word was 100 per cent accurate, and we witnessed God's overflowing presence and supernatural favour on all the preparations for our wedding. Music and the arts had initially brought us together, and we would include these two elements in our wedding ceremony and reception.

As the plans for the wedding were coming together, it was time to move our possessions into our newly rented townhouse. For me, the university year was finished, and we would be moving two households into our future home. Due to Elaine's disability, she could not pack up all her clothes, dishes, and furniture. Friends and family offered to help her pack and move.

All my personal items and furniture were in my basement apartment; however, my friends and family that have helped me move several times will tell you that I have a lot of books, music, and media related items. Instead of hiring a moving company, I decided that we could save this money and move ourselves. Wouldn't you know that, once again, I picked one of the hottest summers on record to coordinate and move these items into our new home? I was a man with a mission, determined to get all our possessions moved and somewhat organized before our wedding. I didn't feel like eating much with such extreme heat temperatures. I was constantly drinking water and missing meals. In the process, I lost twenty-five pounds!

We enjoyed wonderful blessings from our family and friends with many showers and wedding gifts. Elaine is an incredible chef and hostess. Just as a side note … we are a unique team. She plans and then cooks all the food. I take care of the décor, the table settings, the musical selections, and the clean-up!

Elaine recalls our rehearsal party the day before our wedding:

"The rehearsal party on Friday evening came together with everyone learning their position for the ceremony. My father practised walking me down the aisle. As I met Ian at the front of the chapel, my father stepped back and the pastor asked 'Who gives this woman to be married to this man?' After a slight pause— as if thinking it over—my father said, 'My mother and I.'

"At that point, the entire wedding party broke out in hysterical laughter. Previously my father had told us that for two weeks, over and over in his mind, he had been preparing his line and walking me down the aisle. He had that one line and wanted to make sure that he had it down just right.

The next day at the wedding, I was at the back of the church waiting to walk down the aisle to meet Ian. My favourite hymn, 'O Worship the King,' was being played on the organ. Arm in arm, I proceeded to come down the aisle with my father. I know my father and mother were very proud of me that day. On my father's arm, we met Ian at the front of the church. My father presented me to Ian and stepped back. The pastor asked, 'Who gives this woman to marry this man?' Again, a long silent pause. Finally, he said, 'Her mother and I.' My father got it right!"

When Elaine and I first talked about our wedding service, we wanted to make it a Christian celebration of the arts. We wanted many instruments involved in the service—piano, trumpet, guitars, violin, drums, Celtic harp, and voice. We also asked our friends who sang, played, or danced to be His anointed instruments.

We wanted both hymns of the church and Christian contemporary worship songs. We wanted dance and banners to be a part of the celebration. What we didn't plan on was the extremely hot weather. The ceremony took forty-five minutes to an hour in length—without any air conditioning in the church! I wanted two specific selections included in our wedding—one, a choreographed dance piece that would incorporate our personalities, and secondly, just before Elaine came down the aisle, I wanted to serenade my bride with a song. I chose Twila Paris' "How Beautiful."

When I saw Elaine in her wedding dress, she looked so beautiful I could barely hold back the tears. I couldn't have chosen a more perfect song. This song is based on Isaiah 52:7—How beautiful are the feet of them that preach the gospel of peace. This song was my way to speak prophetically to the heavenly hosts (that sometime within our lifetime together) Elaine's total healing would take place!

I wore a white tuxedo jacket to symbolize the biblical priest before the throne of grace, pure and holy before God. Many friends said they could sense God's anointing on me when I sang to Elaine. We both enjoyed God's precious oil of joy flowing around us and on the wedding party throughout the ceremony. The atmosphere was intoxicating, and we were getting very drunk in the Spirit from being in the presence of the Lord.

For my groomsmen I selected Joseph, also known as Pepe, as my Best Man, along with Rick, Gary, and Stewart. Pepe is an anointed drummer and a great friend. Rick and Stewart are members of Elaine's family. Gary and I go way back! Our two families go back more than fifty years. Our grandparents were close friends. Gary and I connected at Camp Kwasind and Baptist youth events. Our dear friends, Cheryl Sebrins and Katherine (Davis) Spannerman, created a beautiful dance piece using flags and banners to the recorded track of Sandi Patty's song, "Artist of My Soul."

Maybe it was the lyrics in this song that led me to think about and research the words "stirring of my soul." As I was thinking, praying, planning, and writing the manuscript for this book, the concept and title "Stirring My Soul to Sing" kept going over and over in my mind, as did the memories of all the journeys and struggles to get to this place during our happiest moments, even on our wedding day. This song "Artist of my Soul" explained so much for me in my spiritual journey and in the understanding of how my ADHD had given me moments of creative joy and a lot of sorrow. Thus the "stirring in soul" continued.

This song, "Artist of my Soul," and our wedding choreographic dance were designed personally for us and watching the video of the dance is still very emotional for both of us. The Holy Spirit inspired them to create a graceful work with beauty and magic interwoven in this dance. I am moved every time we watch this part of our wedding ceremony on DVD. Every year right around our anniversary we try to watch this video. It's our way of remembering, renewing, and committing our vows to each other.

Our wedding day, June 26, 1999. One of my favourite pictures of our special day! (Walker Family Photo Collection)

During our long courtship, we started to write a song for our wedding called, "Now We Are One in You." We would sing it as a duet after our vows. The words are found earlier in this book. Elaine wrote most of the lyrics and music. When we sang this song together at our wedding, I messed up some of the lyrics. I had forgotten to print them out before the wedding. I scrambled just before the service to write them down. As we sang, Elaine raised her eyebrows at me as if to say, "What are you saying? Those aren't the right words!"

The video of this moment is rather cute! "Now We Are One in You" has become a favourite when we perform it in other settings. After our vows, we included Christina in the creation of our new family unit. We gave her a ring of her own, engraved with her initials.

Elaine and I had planned our reception at Crossroads Christian Communications Centre (where *100 Huntley Street* is recorded.) We wanted both family cultures to be involved in the program, so we asked Elaine's brothers and their families to perform. My sister, Janet, gave a very funny speech about our Walker family traditions. Elaine's oldest brother, Rick, spoke on Kawai family traditions and Elaine's many accomplishments. My good friend, Bill Bynum, spoke and warned—or alerted—Elaine to some of my personal "Royal Family idiosyncrasies." Both fathers gave their short speeches and welcomed us respectively into the Kawai and Walker family.

Elaine's mother, Alice, was well connected in the Hamilton Japanese community and arranged to have a Japanese dancer for us (complete with the traditional Japanese costume with fans.) Elaine and I felt like Japanese royalty as Jennifer danced before us while we were seated at the head table. Jennifer concluded her dance, bowing first to us and then to the audience as they applauded very enthusiastically. It was a moving experience, well representing both of our cultures. Our friends and family would enjoy watching the video of this performance. Elaine and I danced our first dance together, and we selected Celine Dion's "Because You Love Me." It was our song from the first of our courtship, and it was right to dance it together as man and wife.

We had arranged for the use of Frank's car to get the bride and groom to their places and to the venue for family pictures and then to the reception hall. However, as we were saying goodbye to our guests, we didn't want the party to end! I then realized my oversight. Oops! We didn't have a ride back to the house, where Elaine's family were having a late-night snack. Angie, one of our friends who had helped us with decorating the tables (with handmade chocolate table favours), lived nearby Elaine's parents. Becoming our impromptu chauffer, she took the newly married couple to the family party. We enjoyed Japanese food and mingled with the relatives. It was close to 2:00 a.m. when Angie offered to take us to our hotel. To make the room very special, I had pre-booked our accommodations and arranged for our pre-packed luggage to be waiting in our room, along with some favourite comforts from home, including our portable CD player.

Then, barely three or four hours later, promptly at 7:00 a.m., Celine Dion's voice came blasting from the CD player. The entire room shook! I had forgotten to turn off the alarm feature on the ghetto box! We roared with laughter, waking up so suddenly—finally together as husband and wife! We reminisced about our personal memories of the special day.

Unable to get back to sleep, we decided to open the gift cards from generous family and friends. As we opened card after card, cash would fall out. For once in our lives we decided we could throw all this money into the air and not worry about a thing. God indeed had been faithful to us in providing everything that we would need for our new home and life together.

CHAPTER TWENTY
THE SOUL STIRRED TO SING AND TO DANCE

When I was a young child, I loved to hear and read the Bible stories of King David. At camp, we once had a special speaker who taught for an entire week about David, the shepherd boy who would be king. Out came the felt board with the different characters illustrating the story of David's life. The speaker set the scene by introducing us to the young boy, David, sitting on a rock, strumming his harp, and worshipping God while tending his flock of sheep. The next lesson presented the story of David, the young man, and Goliath, the giant enemy. Lastly was the account of David's struggle on his journey to rise to the throne as the future king. As a boy, the visual and artistic felt pictures truly brought the Bible stories to life for me.

Now as a man and a prayer warrior, I see that my life and the struggles that I have encountered over these many years are not so different from David's. Only recently I sat down and re-read the biblical text and saw the similarities between our lives. Until then, I'd never thought of my life's story as compared to King David's. David's passionate desire was to be the worshipper and warrior combined. That's my desire as well.

The Worshipper: Just like David, nothing gives me more pleasure than grabbing a portable instrument and worshipping God. My typical favourite is to play my flute up at the cottage, sitting near the docks overlooking the lake. As you will remember from the beginning of this book, without a doubt, my DNA was programmed for ministry.

King David wrote the book of Psalms, first as a child, and witnessed the spiritual realm while singing his love letters of songs and praises. David also learned that he could communicate his feelings to God every day. He wrote and sang about his frustrations through his poetry and music. In Genesis 1:1,3 we read, "*In the beginning God (Elohim) created [by forming from nothing] the heavens and the earth ... And God said, 'Let there be light'; and there was light.*"

God's plan for redemption was given through His spoken word—through His voice. Recently I heard that scientists have discovered that sound waves in the atmosphere pick up and retain the spoken word or letters of the Hebrew language. When these sounds or Hebrew texts are spoken and recorded and then played over and over, it has been documented that great healing has been brought to the physical body, mind, and soul. Alyosha Ryabinov, a Russian classical musician and pianist, was once an atheist. Now a believer, he shares his testimony about how natural sounds and the Hebrew language can produce physical healing to the body through music:

Vibrations create and change substance. I recently composed a CD entitled, *The Lord Is My Healer*. Scriptures read in Hebrew accompany the music. It's amazing because people are being touched in their spirits although they may not understand the Hebrew language. Interestingly, a Swiss physician and scientist, Hans Jenny, constructed an instrument called a tonoscope to make sound visible on substances like water or sand. Different shapes appeared on the sand as the result of different sounds coming through the device. He then tried spoken words in different languages but nothing happened.

When he spoke the Hebrew language, however, the language spoken made the shapes of Hebrew vowels on the sand. None of the modern languages did that. Although Hans Jenny was not a Christian, I accept the science of his research. I believe that when God spoke the universe into existence, the sound of His voice set in motion frequencies that became shapes. In fact, many scientists believe that everything in this universe is made of sound. Today, when we align our thoughts with the thoughts of God and speak them out, the creative power of God goes forth to accomplish that which He desires.

That is why I believe that when the healing Scriptures are spoken in Hebrew it makes an imprint, not only on our mind, but also on our cells for we are made of dust (sand). This is the glorious focus the Lord is directing us in with music and the spoken Word of God for such a time as this! It is the understanding of this Quantum Faith Science, which God is granting to us with sound, frequency, vibration, and the manifestation of matter. It has to do with creationism, the formation of entire planetary solar systems being created by the sound of the Voice—God's Word![12]

God's voice is out there! Through the release of His sound waves, His voice is available for all to see, hear, and experience. He is proving to man once again that His true power of the spoken word releases healing and is available for all! If only one will totally believe and trust in Him.

I also love the continuing part of the story of David when he danced before the Ark of the Covenant and before Yahweh-God. David is only wearing his ephod, described as a long undershirt from the top of his neck to the bottoms of his feet. He wore no other kingly regalia or tailor-made clothing during his praise and worship times before the God of Abraham, Isaac, and Jacob! At contrasting times in his life, David was stripped bare

---

[12] Alyosha Ryabinov, "Hebrew: The Language of Heaven," *Sid Roth's It's Supernatural and Messianic Vision*, https://sidroth.org/newsletter/march-2007-newsletter/ (accessed April 2, 2018).

of everything-his dignity, his position, his wealth, his impending throne and later the respect of his children and his heirs. Having experienced the absolute vulnerability of being stripped down to nothing, was it any wonder that David wanted nothing to come between him and his God when he intimately worshiped Him?

As a shepherd boy, God anointed him to become king and assume his rightful place on the throne of Israel. Then he would have to wait seven years until the transformation to become, David of Israel. David's wife despised him, dancing out there in his underwear! In her opinion, he was not setting a good example of his kingly role. But David didn't care. Anyone with a negative and prideful attitude would not block his passion from intimately being in God's presence.

I have a keen sensitivity toward injustice. Seeing loved ones or races of people imprisoned for their beliefs makes me weep. I've recently watched the film *Mandela: A Long Walk to Freedom*. I didn't know all the biographical information about Nelson Mandela, and I found this film very moving and enlightening. What struck me the most about Mandela's character was shown after his imprisonment. He had the ability to forgive his jailers and then to encourage his people that non-violence was the only way that he, his party, and the black South African people could make significant changes to their long walk to freedom. David also forgave Saul for all the injustice that was dealt to him, and he wouldn't touch Saul's garment when he was so close he could have easily taken out his adversary. David chose non-violence and to let God resolve the difficult issues between them.

In my life, there are walls that I cannot climb or destroy. There are barriers of wrong impressions and attitudes about me that I cannot scale or change, so I've learned to preserve my inner peace; I must turn these negative thoughts and emotional junk over to the Lord. He is my defender and advocate. I have decided that for the rest of my life, I will not allow my natural body to enter this level of emotional stress or judgement. I've taken a bold stance that through forgiveness and trust in God, I will not allow strife or worry to enter my mind and wreak havoc through sickness, disease, and confusion in my spirit! In times of confusion, I choose to focus on praising Him for everything that we need and for the many blessings that Papa God has given.

Earlier, I shared with you the impacting word of the Lord that the late Jill Austin of Master Potter Ministries spoke over me. That prophetic utterance still makes me tremble and shake. I am very serious when I think about the responsibility that the Lord has given me in releasing the prophetic arts and its mantle to this current and next generation. Through Jill's book, *Dancing with Destiny*, I came to realise that God had given her the same theme to explore: worshipping and warfare. I like what Dutch Sheets says about this topic from the foreword of Jill's book:

> In this enjoyable book, Jill marries two enigmatic pieces of our destiny: worshipping and warring. She calls our dance with destiny the dance of a warrior. You are not just a dreamer and a lover, she declares. You are a warrior! She is right-we have become the enigma. We are the generation of those who seek Him, who seek Your face (Psalms 24.6) and those who declare that our God is the Lord strong and mighty, the Lord mighty in battle (verse 8). We are worshipping warriors, loving liberators. There are some in the world who try to brand Christians as radicals who want to control everything. How wrong they are! We know what we are: we are freedom fighters on a mission of mercy.[13]

I know what it's like to be considered a dreamer and a warrior stripped of everything! I know what it's like to experience every convenience or financial resource denied. These are the times of testing, the times to learn to be totally dependent upon God. I have an idea of the pain that David felt when he would cry, petition, and ask God to move on his behalf on a point of urgency. I too know what it's like to be a warrior for one's causes and beliefs!

As I have shared with you throughout the many chapters of my story, I needed to go through some of these painful desert experiences, and to feel at times that Heaven wasn't listening. Elaine and I now know of God's true

---

[13] Jill Austin, *Dancing with Destiny* (Grand Rapids: Chosen Books, 2007), 12.

love-plan for us and of His compassion. His definitive plan for us includes blessings and prosperity, but I also have to realize that for God's plan to become our lives, God's anointing comes at great personal cost. When one is released into God's special calling and ministry, it can only come through Him. Placement and promotion only come by waiting on God.

From the lowest valleys to highest spiritual encounters with God, this destiny is my calling as worshipper, musician, and arts consultant. Elaine is being brought forward in her gifting of healing, evangelism, and in teaching and releasing the Word of God. These revelations were revealed and prophesied to both of us over time; however, only now are they beginning to produce fruit. We both have learned the hard way that we simply needed to get our fleshly selves out of the way and let God have His way.

I have received many blessed moments of revelation by just giving it all to God. We have experienced going higher and higher in the realm of the Holy Spirit. The presence, the power, and the depth of God are tangible. You feel like the room is about to explode as it fills up more and more with the presence of God. Some sense the presence of angels, some see angels, and others feel the sweet and cooling presence of the Holy Spirit. Now in my fifties, I think that I understand, just a bit, how God wants to get my attention through these amazing and supernatural encounters with Him.

Elaine and I have been pressing into Him, soaking in His anointing, and the most amazing things have been happening in the supernatural realm. As I shared with you earlier, when I was a child, Jesus revealed Himself to me. Then at the age of sixteen, I had Samuel-like experiences of God calling me by name three times. Later, there was the wheel of fire, an open vision. These Holy Ghost encounters have continued. They seem to be the most real when we are desperate. God just wants us to focus on Him. I love being in His glory and watching the Holy Spirit move around the room. You can sense that there are healings taking place and God is speaking! As a worshipper, I love being a carrier of His glory.

The Warrior: I love the story of David and Goliath, especially when David would not listen to Goliath blaspheming God. David knew who He was in God and his limited abilities as a shepherd boy. He reached for those five smooth stones in his bag and then placed the first one in his slingshot and struck Goliath in the centre of his forehead. Goliath fell over dead! There have been many Goliaths that I have had to confront to get where God wants me to be today. Like Joseph, the dreamer, people would often scoff and mock me. They would tell me that I was in a world of fancy and imagination. I would be as courteous as possible and reply with a smile. Even in my teenage life I was learning to listen to God and receive His instructions.

It takes learning to be sensitive to the Holy Spirit's voice and not murmur. During times of emotional upheaval, as the priest of my home today, I need to be the warrior to claim spiritual territory for my family to stand firm. God has instructed me to use His weapons of warfare, which includes my anointed flag (with the Lion of Judah in the centre surrounded by four trumpets to proclaim victory). The enemy has no right to be meddling in God's and my business!

I raise the flag as a signal. I speak out verbally the words that Jesus used ("It is written") to inform the enemy to back off. I like the scripture verse which says: *All you inhabitants of the world, you who dwell on the earth, when a signal is raised on the mountains-look! When a trumpet is blown-hear!* (Isaiah 18:3) It is a declaration of war, combined with praise, worship and thanksgiving to God. I encourage you to do the same. If you have made Jesus Christ the personal Lord and Saviour of your life, you have the authority to tell the enemy that he is under your feet! (Romans 16:19–20)

Lastly, I need to share with you that I have been mentally and physically healed of my ADHD. Through a series of "God encounters" I was radically healed of this disorder. Combining all the "healthy, non-medicated options," such as going through many hours of Christian counselling and spending many hours in praise and worship (these are my intimate times with God), I found freedom. I also forgave myself and others who deeply hurt me. I now have a different perception of myself and in the way that "I think or process about a situation;" it is not wrong…it is my authentic thought process!

I also re-gained my self-esteem to complete projects (such as my university education) that I was fearful to get-back on track, due to my

ADHD hang-ups. Within time, I completed and received my BA. I also have a new image of myself- as God sees me ... as His cherished and blessed son! Even today, Elaine and I are very involved, active and our opinions, wisdom and leadership skills are valued in our home church. These "wholeness" factors have continued and maintained my healing issues with my ADHD.

Today I experience the total healing of God encapsulating my mind, spirit, and soul. The journey of my new life with Elaine and our marriage continues, and God has blessed us abundantly! During my quiet times before the Lord, He told me that I was to write this book.

Now that my spirit, soul, and mind have been totally healed, I soar and fly like an eagle in the heavens. As the Scripture says: "*But they that wait upon the Lord shall renew their strength; they shall mount up with wings as eagles; they shall run ... and not faint*" (Isaiah 40: 31, KJV). My spirit has been stirred and I sing to Him!

My heart's desire is for you to be inspired to be healed as you read my story. WARNING! You alone have the choice as to what you settle for in your life!

CHAPTER TWENTY-ONE
COME ON IN—THE DOOR IS OPEN!

Transformation can take place when you've surrendered your spirit, heart, mind, and soul totally to God. If you have a disorder, such as ADD/ADHD, everything is all mixed in your thinking. You wonder if God can help. There is a glorious light and there is a freedom ahead, but you need to pursue them.

Take it from me and believe what I am saying. Only through coming to Jesus and maintaining a personal and daily relationship with Him did I find the strength and trust to leave my life; strangling darkness and its issues were left behind. Thus, today I am walking in complete healing.

God loves you and offers a wonderful plan for your life. The beginning step is called salvation—God's gift to whoever wants to receive it. Sometimes it's called the new birth or being born again. Salvation is God's answer to that deep human longing for satisfaction, purpose, and intimacy with the Father. Understanding the heart of the Father, you realize that He is a great and mighty God who desires a relationship with you!

Here's how it works:

God's Plan: "*For God so [greatly] loved and dearly prized the world, that He [even] gave His [One and] only begotten Son, so that whoever believes and trusts in Him [as Savior] shall not perish, but have eternal life. For God did not send the Son into the world to judge and condemn the world [that is, to initiate the final judgment of the world] but that the world might be saved through Him*" (John 3:16–17)

God's Pathway (Jesus is speaking): "*I came that they may have and enjoy life, and have it in abundance [to the full, till it overflows]*" (John 10:10b).

God's Provision: "*But God clearly shows and proves His own love for us, by the fact that while we were still sinners, Christ died for us*" (Romans 5:8).

God's Promise: "*… Christ died for our sins according to [that which] the Scriptures [foretold], and that He was buried, and that He was [bodily] raised on the third day according to [that which] the Scriptures [foretold], and that He appeared to Cephas (Peter), then to the Twelve. After that He appeared to more than five hundred brothers and sisters …*" (1 Corinthians 15:3–6).

God's Present: "*For it is by grace [God's remarkable compassion and favor drawing you to Christ] that you have been saved [actually delivered from judgment and given eternal life] through faith. And this [salvation] is not of yourselves [not through your own effort], but it is the [undeserved, gracious] gift of God; not as a result of [your] works [nor your attempts to keep the Law], so that no one will [be able to] boast or take credit in any way [for his salvation]*" (Ephesians 2:8–9).

God's Purpose: "*But to as many as did receive and welcome Him, He gave the right [the authority, the privilege] to become children of God, that is, to those who believe (adhere to, trust in, rely on) His name …*" (John 1:12).

If your heart has been stirred with the desire for this free gift of a new life and healing in Christ Jesus, I invite you to pray the following: God, I come to you in the name of Jesus. I realize that however hard I try, I cannot save myself. All my good deeds don't measure up when compared to Your holiness. So God, I come to You, on the basis of what Jesus Christ has done for me. Right now, I invite You, Lord Jesus, to come into my life as my Saviour and Lord. Thank you, Jesus, for taking my place and dying on the cross for my sins. Thank you for forgiving all my sins and giving me eternal life.

Thank you for forgiving my sins and living inside of me. I open the door of my heart and receive You, Lord Jesus. I need You! Make me the kind of person you want me to be. Heal me in all the areas of my life. Amen.

The Bible says, "… *everyone who calls upon the name of the Lord ,… shall be saved*" (Acts 2:21). You may also want to review Romans 10:9–10.

Welcome! Come on in! If you would like to call someone and receive any help or clarification concerning your decision, you may call either *100 Huntley Street* in Canada at 1-877-273-4444 or The 700 Club at 1-800-700-7000 in the United States. If you prefer, email me at encounters@emliancommunications.org. May God richly bless you!

"Stirring My Soul to Sing"

VERSE ONE

Born with an affliction that haunted me,
Something that I couldn't control.
The taunting and teasing continued throughout my life;
At times, I just wanted to disappear …
Like Joseph, I was stuck and put in a pit,
Wanting and waiting to be released.
Worshipping you, Lord, you gave me the key,
And now I have the freedom to sing.

CHORUS

Stirring my soul to sing, let the music and melody ring;
As a bird with a wounded wing,
I'm no longer afraid from what life brings,
I'm healed, I'm restored, and I'm ready … to sing.

VERSE TWO

As a man who's growing older,
Accepting the choices of my life,
Some paths were good and some that tested me.
Embracing the ones who love me dear,
Jesus, you loved me in good and bad times.
Mistakes made, and words said in spoken fear,
Now I'm healed to praise and worship you.
Open, my heart and give me more … more of you!
(Yes, you're)

CHORUS

"CREATIVE IMPRESSIONS"
HOW TO PUT THESE LESSONS TO WORK FOR YOU

Throughout the latter chapters of this book, I thought of some questions that you may want to reflect upon, possibly through journaling. Some of these questions were taken from the longer chapters in the book. Explore these thoughts and ideas on your own!

Chapter Ten: What new relationships, contacts, or friendships has God put into your hands? How are you developing these relationships? One of my strengths, despite my disability, is that I became a people person, and networking guru. How about you? What untapped resources have been placed in your pathway?

Chapter Eleven: Have you ever had a supernatural experience with God? How did it change you? After my unique "encounter with God," my life completely changed. I learned that I could totally trust Him to reshape me into a man of God. How about you?

Chapter Twelve: Is there someone in your life (e.g. artists, sports heroes, or business people) who you admire and with whom you want to connect? For me, God used these individuals as bridges to wholeness. I love the scripture verse that my friend, Nancy Honeytree, referred to from Proverbs 18:16: *"A man's gift [given in love or curtesy] makes room for him and brings him before great men."*

Chapter Sixteen: When you've committed yourself to the Lord's work and are obedient to His commandments, God will reward you with His abundant blessings and personal attention to details that only He and you know about! Our story of courtship and marriage is unique. Both of us were disabled and broken. God has been healing and restoring His image in us. It's been totally amazing and life giving! What is your story? How did God bring a special friend into your life?

***

The following Order of Canada Levels of Distinction are referred to throughout the book: Companion of the Order of Canada (C.C), Officer of the Order of Canada (O.C), and Member of the Order of Canada (C.M).

ECG Photos (Emlian Communications Group) which is W. Ian Walker's company.

BIOGRAPHY OF
W. IAN WALKER
—ARTS CONSULTANT, MUSICIAN AND AUTHOR

W. Ian Walker's mission is to be a positive role model for adults and children who have ADHD. Although Ian was told he had a learning disability in the early 1970s, he was not formally diagnosed with the disorder until 1996. In the intervening years, Ian experienced verbal abuse, school bullying, poor academic performance, employment instability, financial hardships, and failed relationships.

Despite the challenges, he persevered and now holds a BA in Theatre and Film from McMaster University and a post-graduate Certificate in Fundraising and Volunteer Management from Humber College, Toronto. Mr. Walker is a successful arts consultant with over thirty years of experience. In the summer of 2016, Ian graduated from Mid-America Christian University's Christian Worship Arts and Leadership Program with their online program. Grammy and Dove Award winning gospel artist Sandi Patty has been the founder and artist in residence to this program.

A high-achieving ADHD survivor, Ian serves as testament to countless ADHD sufferers that *music can do a better job of improving their lives than medicine.* In fact, Ian will share with your audience that music saved his life and "cured him" of his disorder. This music man and arts professional takes audiences behind the lyrics, melodies, and ovations in his book to lay bare the practical lessons he has learned in coping with ADHD for over fifty years.

In spite of his learning disability, throughout the 1990s, Ian continued to pursue his dream of promoting the Christian contemporary music genre (CCM) to its Canadian and international audiences. He was involved in many projects with producing, writing, and broadcasting for Christian tele-vision networks and interviewing some of CCM's legends, such as Sandi Patty, Ralph Carmichael, the late Andrae Crouch, Randy Stonehill, Phil Driscoll, Steven Curtis Chapman, Steve Green, Mark Lowry and Cindy Morgan.

In the fall of 2005, Ian became the founder, music director, and conductor of the newly-formed Youth Choir for the Nations Canada. The Youth Choir sings in English, French, Spanish, and Urdu. During the 2006 Christmas season, the choir participated with international Christian artist, Nancy Honeytree Miller and appeared on *100 Huntley Street*, a national Canadian Christian television program. Nancy Honeytree has since become a friend to both Ian and Elaine Walker and authored the Foreword to this book.

Ian & Elaine Walker have been members of Catch the Fire Ministry (formerly TACF) and Partners in Harvest Ministry for over twenty years and have been "so blessed" by all of the friendships, ministry connections, and resourceful servants of God who have been a part of their lives since they were married.

For more information, please contact W. Ian Walker, Emlian Communications Group, at encounters@emliancommunications.org.

W. Ian Walker, President/CEO

Emlian Communications Group Inc.

P. O. Box 60508

Hamilton, ON, Canada L9C 7N7

WORKS CITED

Austin, Jill. *Dancing with Destiny.* Grand Rapids, MI: Chosen Books, 2007.

Bail, Nina. *Through It All: Andrae Crouch.* Waco, Tx: Word Books, 1974.

Bunyan, John. *The Pilgrim's Progress: From This World to That Which Is to Come, Delivered under the Similitude of a Dream.* Ware: Wordsworth Editions, 1996.

Chambers, Oswald. *My Utmost for His Highest* (revised). Grand Rapids, MI: Discovery House Publishers, 2008.

Colbert, Dr. Don. *Deadly Emotions.* Nashville: W Publishing Group, 2006.

Fonda, Jane. *My Life so Far.* Toronto: Random House, 2005.

Hurnard, Hannah. *Hinds' Feet on High Places.* UK: Christian Literature Crusade, 1955.

Kaufman, Scott Barry. "The Creative Gifts of ADHD." *Scientific American.* Accessed April 2, 2018. https://blogs.scientificamerican.com/beautiful-minds/the-creative-gifts-of-adhd/.

Owen, William (ed.). *A Life in Music: Conversations with Sir David Willcocks and Friends.* New York, NY: Oxford University Press, 2008.

Rodgers, Anni Layne. "Music Therapy: Sound Medicine for ADHD." *ADDitude: Inside the ADHD Mind.* Accessed April 2, 2018. https://www.additudemag.com/music-therapy-for-adhd-how-rhythm-builds-focus/.

Ryabinov, Alyosha. "Hebrew: The Language of Heaven." *Sid Roth's It's Supernatural and Messianic Vision.* Accessed April 2, 2018. https://sidroth.org/newsletter/march-2007-newsletter/.

Walker, W. Ian. "The Handshake That Changed My Life." *Preludes, Fugues and Riffs.* Fall/Winter (2002): 5.

Walton, Donald. *A Rockwell Portrait: An Intimate Biography.* Kansas City: Sheed Andrews and McMeel, 1978.